WHAT SMART PEOPLE DO WHEN LOSING THEIR JOBS

WHAT SMART PEOPLE DO
WHEN
LOSING THEIR JOBS

Kathleen A. Riehle

John Wiley and Sons, Inc.

New York • Chichester • Brisbane • Toronto • Singapore

Library of Congress Cataloging-in-Publication Data
Riehle, Kathleen, A. 1961–
    What smart people do when losing their jobs / by Kathleen A. Riehle.
        p.   cm.
    Includes bibliographical references and index.
    ISBN 0-471-55081-7.—ISBN 0-471-55082-5 (pbk.)
    1. Employees—Dismissal of.   2. Professional employees—
Psychology.   3. Unemployment.   4. Job hunting.   I. Title.
HF5549.5.D55R54   1991
650.14—dc20   91-13338

Printed in the United States of America

10 9 8 7 6 5 4 3 2 1

To my husband, Barry,
who really meant it
when he said,
"for better or worse."

Acknowledgments

I'd like to acknowledge Michael Hamilton for taking a chance.

Many thanks to the Public Library of Cincinnati and Hamilton County for patient research assistance.

Sincere thanks also to my experts, Daniel Averbeck, Ph.D., Eileen Raffaniello, Ph.D., Marlene Schmidt, M.D., and Donald Sheehan of the Ohio Bureau of Employment Services.

For technical support, I'd also like to thank Matthew Rich of Rich Associates Technical Services.

Special thanks to some good people who have lived through some difficult times. Their stories helped me write this book and will, I hope, help others deal with the impact of job loss.

Contents

Introduction   1

1   Anticipating a Layoff   5

2   The Day You Find Out   23

3   The Emotional Impact   36

4   For the Understanding Spouse   54

5   The Unemployment Office   74

6   Family Financial Security   94

7   Surviving Up to a Year Without an Income   115

8   Looking for a Job   131

9   Honey, I Found a Job!   162

Index   177

WHAT SMART PEOPLE DO
WHEN
LOSING THEIR JOBS

Introduction

"I went numb. I could not say anything for a minute." That's how one middle manager of a brewing company described his reaction to the news that he was being laid off after 13 years with the company. They sent someone back to clean out his office and give him his personal items. Like this man, most people describe the experience of losing a job as a "huge psychological blow."

According to a *Wall Street Journal* article, layoffs and the "pervasive fear" of dismissal create intense stress in the workplace. When a Citibank unit announced plans to lay off 2000 people, two employees committed suicide. Chase Manhattan Corp. recently planned to eliminate 12 percent of its workforce. Digital Equipment Corp., the largest employer in Massachusetts, planned to reduce its 120,000-person employee population by 3000. An analyst suggested that the company needed to lose many times that many employees to become efficient by industry standards.

That's the bad news. In fact, this is a bad news/good news book. The other side of the story is that a great many people not only survive job loss but ultimately experience positive effects that help them in their careers and personal lives. Many of the most successful people have at one time or another experienced the loss of a job.

Camille Lavington, an international career consultant, says, "If you haven't been fired, you aren't real. We are going through a social revolution in the professional business world. In the past few years people have become more sophisticated and understanding about people moving from one job to another. It's accepted in a way it never was. Corporate loyalty is gone. To be let out of a company is no longer a stigma."

Some people even point to job loss as a key reason for their future successes. Larry Betsinger, a top information systems executive interviewed by *Computerworld* magazine, believes, "the only way I got to being a big shot and making lots of money was because I got fired." Many other people point to a job loss or layoff as a turning point in their career, one that eventually led to bigger and better things.

The good news is that you can be in control of the situation. You can be aware and anticipate possible job loss. You can prepare yourself and your family for the possibility of a layoff. In the event that it happens, you can learn to deal with the emotional and financial stress and survive the experience with valuable lessons that will make you more effective at the office and happier at home.

This book is a guide for anyone who is concerned about losing a job, or for those who have already been informed their positions are being eliminated. As you read the stories of others who have experienced job loss, you'll realize that they have survived and grown professionally and personally from the experience. The simple, logical advice in each chapter will help you manage your financial situation and deal with the emotional impact of losing your job.

This book will also help you realize that Camille Lavington is right. A great many "real" people lose their jobs. You aren't the only one who feels the concern, the worry, and the loss of self-esteem. As you read the stories of others who have experienced exactly what you are experiencing, you'll realize, as they did, that you still have worth, both to your family and to potential new employers.

As you read this book, you may identify with one or more sections more strongly than with others. If you have recently experienced job loss, this reaction will be typical. Many psychologists agree that job loss is similar to the breakup of a marriage or the loss of a loved one. The emotional impact can be just as strong. The added burden of new financial worries compounds your struggle.

If the person suffering job loss is someone close to you, especially a spouse, this book will help you understand what he or she is feeling and will help you continue to be supportive through what may be an equally devastating experience for you. For the spouse of someone out of work, it's definitely one of the "bad times" you vowed to be faithful through. The important thing to realize is that the good times do return and that from the experience you and your spouse will gain valuable lessons that can bring you and your family closer together.

One note about the information in the book: This book isn't intended as a "how-to" guide to job searches or resumé writing. Books on those topics abound, and I have mentioned some of the helpful ones in Chapter 8. Rather than duplicate general information on job searches, the job-search material in this book is tailored to the specific situation of someone currently out of work and looking for a new position.

Finally, if you've never lost a job but are still concerned, the most important piece of advice this book has to offer is the old Boy Scout adage, *be prepared*. You know that the odds of a natural disaster striking your home are relatively small, yet every member of your family knows how to deal with the potential dangers involved. The odds of losing your job at one point or another during your career are at least as great as the odds that a natural calamity will befall you. With the ever-changing uncertainty in today's economic and business environments, doesn't it make sense to at least be prepared?

1 | Anticipating a Layoff

On a gray March afternoon, the president of a small magazine publishing company called everyone into the company's only conference room for a short meeting. After weeks of rumors about declining advertising revenues and a downturn in the economy, most employees feared the worst. The company's few top managers had had several closed-door meetings over the last two weeks.

"I'm out of here, I know it," Marlene, an editor, recalls thinking. She was lowest on the seniority list and had less overall experience than one or two others in her department. The president seemed distracted and tense. He looked at the ceiling every few seconds and cleared his throat several times, as if looking for words.

"I know you've all been hearing rumors about our current situation," he began. "I'm here today to tell you that there is no cause for worry. Yes, ad revenues are down, but we don't plan any immediate changes. We have some plans in place to help increase our revenues. We'll wait until after the first of the year and then reassess our position."

"I was relieved," Marlene remembers. "I knew he seemed

5

agitated and worried, but I really believed he meant what he said."

Three days later, the editor and three of her colleagues were laid off with two weeks' severance pay.

A generation ago, the "company man" myth was a reality. People could join a company straight out of high school or college, put in their 30 years, and retire with a safe pension. Somewhere in the middle of OPEC oil shortages, global competition, "stagflation," and supply-side economics, the company man disappeared. From the highest-paid vice president to the people driving the delivery trucks, no one's job will ever again be considered safe.

In the past several years, it has also become clearer that management jobs are at stake now more than ever. Companies that have experienced decades of growth now find themselves with huge middle-management ranks and declining profitability. In the last two decades, many companies have gone from having close to 49 management employees for every 100 non-managers to more than 59 managers for every 100 non-managers. Some huge companies have experienced an even greater growth in middle-management positions. Management experts are now advocating "demassification," a high-tech term synonymous with layoffs of hundreds or thousands of middle managers.

A desire to be more "Japanese" is also fueling the fire. Many American companies want to "slim down" by trimming the number of levels of management under which they currently operate. Some companies have 10 or 11 separate levels of management, while management consultants suggest that 4 to 6 may be a more efficient and manageable structure.

The critical question in an era of increasing employment insecurity is: How do I know if my job is safe? More importantly: What are the signs that my company may be thinking of letting me go?

Two common threads run through the stories of people who have lost their jobs: First, no matter how important you think you are to the company, any one of a number of factors may make you expendable. Second, in difficult economic times there are several significant warning signs that layoffs in general are on the way and that you may be on the list. These warning signs can be the key to your future. You can learn to read them and respond when you see them.

THE EARLY WARNING SIGNS

A pending layoff is like car trouble—before anything drastic happens, you usually experience a few knocks and pings. If you understand your car well, you can read the noises to know if something serious needs repair. With a little proactive effort, you can avoid being stranded at the side of the road. When a company is in trouble, it emits knocks and pings of its own. You'll find some of the more obvious noises, and some not-so-obvious ones, described below.

Bad News Travels Fast

One of the most obvious early warning signs to watch for is specific mention of your company's situation in the press. If you work for a large company, these signs will be prominently displayed in publications such as the *Wall Street Journal* or other business or trade publications. Often, news of rapidly falling revenues or rapidly rising losses is a sure indicator that the corporation is planning layoffs. Leaks of planned layoffs often reach the trade press long before individuals actually receive notice. The more you read, the better prepared you will be for the inevitable consequences of a failing business.

According to Robert Tomasco, an expert on corporate downsizing, "One response many companies made to their stalemated growth prospects was to shift attention from market share to stock price as the key indicator of performance. This 'value-based planning' has led to a breakup of many conglomerates when they determine that the price-earnings multiple of their stocks is being held back by one or two lackluster divisions."

The result, according to Tomasco, is that a division of a large company may be forced to stand on its own. The cold light of day outside the safe environment of the corporate parent can result in numerous layoffs when the new organization realizes just how inefficient it really has become.

Forewarning of announcements such as these generally appears in widely circulated publications. If you work for a company whose stock is publicly traded, something as simple as watching your company's stock price and earnings numbers can give you an obvious but important clue. Below is an excerpt from an article that appeared in the *Wall Street Journal* in February 1991:

Pratt & Whitney Says By July It Will Cut 1,000 to 1,500 Jobs

NEW YORK—Pratt & Whitney, citing the airline industry's weakened state, said it will eliminate between 1,000 and 1,500 jobs in the U.S. in the first half of this year.

The decision accelerates a plan announced last August to eliminate 4,000 jobs, or 11% of its domestic work force, by 1993. At that time, the jet engine unit of United Technologies Corp. blamed the planned layoffs on military spending cuts.

The company said layoffs will begin next month, with most of the cuts occurring in Connecticut, where most of its production is done. Smaller reductions will take place in Maine, Georgia and Florida. Since August, Pratt & Whitney has reduced its work force by 700 through attrition.

The article goes on to say that Pratt & Whitney's spare parts business makes up one-third of its overall revenues and that this part of the business has been severely hurt by a downturn in the airline industry. You can see that if you had been reading the *Journal* all along, you probably would have already been aware of the factors leading up to this recent decision.

Losing the Big One

The Bureau of Labor Statistics lists "contract completion" as one of the most frequent causes of layoffs. Companies, especially small ones, often hire employees to fulfill a large contract they've recently won. The logic is always expansionist and optimistic: Once we finish this one, there will be others like it; we'll be able to keep these people busy. But often the contract is just a one-time lucky break, or the company or agency awarding the contract decides to cancel or re-bid it. In any event, rapid expansion in response to "the big sale" inevitably leads to layoffs if and when the contract is completed or rescinded for whatever reason.

Layoffs due to unexpected changes in major contracts are sometimes difficult to foresee. The best way to stay informed is to form a good working relationship with the people who are most aware of possible changes in large contracts: either the account executive who "landed the big one" or the program or project manager responsible for managing contract completion. By maintaining at least a casual, conversational relationship with these individuals, you may pick up on disturbing trends that lead you to believe the contract may be changed or canceled.

Managed Attrition

Managed attrition is a business euphemism that can mean, "Whew, there's one more we won't have to let go." Especially when a company is large, before its management tries any sort of whole-scale layoff, they may hope that careful attention to attrition and hiring will ease financial concerns. If your company suddenly becomes stingy in its hiring plans, this could be a sign that the problem is greater than it appears on the surface.

Signs to watch for here include cancellations of open personnel requisitions and attempts to retrain personnel for other tasks. You may have had an open request for a new analyst, only to find that your request has been canceled, leaving you to pick up the slack. Or your company may start trying to train accountants to be programmers rather than hire additional programming talent. Any of these signs show that the company is extremely concerned about head count, a situation that can lead management to try other means of reducing its payroll.

Merger Mania

Although the trend slowed after the merger-crazy 1980s, large mergers and acquisitions usually produce redundant positions within the new, merged company. Again, the best way to watch for signs of a potential merger or acquisition are to read trade publications. You may begin to realize a pattern in your industry, or you may even find articles reporting on specific rumors about your company.

Immediate plans for a merger or acquisition should be a cause for concern. Even if the merged organization is extremely successful, some jobs may need to be eliminated simply because their functions are redundant. If the merger is less than successful, many more jobs may be on the line as the new company attempts to reduce debt incurred as part of the merger. When Sperry Corp. and Burroughs Corp. were joined in one of the largest-ever computer industry mergers, the new company had lofty goals of giving industry giant IBM a run for its money. Instead, the new company stumbled. By the end of 1990, Unisys had fewer employees than Sperry Corp. alone had had before the merger.

What Are They Doing behind Those Closed Doors?

In the five years he worked for an entrepreneurial specialty chemicals manufacturer, Frank, a chemical engineer, recalls that the company went through more than a half-dozen layoffs. Each one was preceded by a series of long, closed-door meetings involving the top management of the company and a few other key managers. Meeting participants would often emerge tense and stern from these long sessions spent deciding who stayed and who went. Each time, those not involved in these meetings were aware of exactly what was happening. They waited "downstairs," creating their own whispered guesses of who they thought was "on the list."

"The worst part was knowing what was going on. It just seemed to go on forever," Frank related. "Because engineers were pretty much in demand most of the time, I usually didn't worry. But the rest of the company stopped dead during those times. Everyone knew what was going on, and the attitude was, 'Hey, if they're going to lay me off, why should I break my back meeting deadlines?' "

In larger companies, the process is much the same. If you are employed at the corporate headquarters, your department manager or director may be called into a series of closed-door meetings unrelated to specific projects for which he or she currently has responsibility. Directors or managers of branch or satellite offices may be called to the corporate headquarters more frequently than usual, with little or no explanation for the sudden spate of extra meetings. One key piece of advice: If your manager or director returns from one of these meetings and can't seem to look you in the eye or is obviously uncomfortable talking with you, get your resumé together. You're probably on the list.

Frank said, "My boss was the *worst* person when it came to laying people off. He'd come out of those meetings looking like someone just ran over his cat. You could tell he just hated that part of the job. He'd walk past someone in the hall, and just by the way he acted you could tell if the guy was on the list. It was a creepy feeling if he didn't look you in the eye."

We've Never Had This Many Company Meetings Before

Often when a business is having financial problems, company management will be concerned about panic and defections among the employee population. Even if they are planning to lay off several workers or several thousand workers, the management of the company will be concerned that the right people stay or go. Often they will be concerned that talented or highly valuable employees will get nervous about the situation and decide to start looking for a more stable position with a more financially sound company. As a result, the management of a financially troubled company will often use general memos or company meetings to try to calm the growing sense of anxiety among the general population.

This type of "everything's okay" meeting is analogous to the owner of a professional sports team being "100 percent behind the coach" during a losing season. Because the team's management wants to keep some semblance of order among the players, the owner will ardently and often tell the press, "He's our coach for the future, and we're 100 percent behind him." At the same time, the team management is likely to be scrambling in the background, trying to find someone to replace the guy they're about to fire. If it looks as though your company is currently losing badly, but your management insists there is nothing wrong, it may be a sign that there is more going on than they are ready to disclose.

Marlene, the editor mentioned earlier in this chapter, believes this was the case in her situation. Because the company was small, its rumor mill was well developed and working overtime at the time of the layoff. The magazine had a technical focus, which would make it difficult to replace some of the more experienced writers or editors who might choose to leave for a more secure environment. The company's goal in having an "everything's okay" meeting was to ensure that the right people stayed when the company chose to downsize.

The memory of this meeting was particularly difficult for Marlene during the six months she was out of work. "I felt so gullible," she said. "I should have watched his *face* instead of listening to what he was saying. That meeting has made it difficult for me to trust people in business situations."

Such a meeting can be an important sign that you need to move quickly. Marlene's situation was somewhat unusual because the company acted so soon after the meeting. In most instances, you will have more than one or two days to prepare. However, when your company is in financial trouble, it's never too soon to start. One positive aspect of these meetings is that they bring the company's situation out in the open. By acknowledging the rumors, your manager unknowingly opens the door for you to discuss the company's situation in more detail with him or her. Such an open discussion may allow you to read between the lines and gather information that can help you. For more information on how to be proactive in this situation, see "Making Your Case" later in this chapter.

The Incredible Shrinking Paycheck

A business that is losing money will often try a variety of cost-cutting measures before laying off any employees. One strategy often employed is an across-the-board pay cut or pay deferral. The pay cut or deferral may also take the form of cancellation of earned vacation, vacation deferrals, or short-term "vacations without pay" for some or all of the employee population. Such plans are based on the hope that by slightly reducing everyone's pay, no one will have to be out of work altogether. Sometimes the tactic works; more often it is a harbinger of outright layoffs in the near future.

"Before the layoffs they tried all kinds of cost-cutting measures in the beginning," said Frank, "with the most drastic being an across-the-board 15 percent pay cut. I think they hoped some people would leave on their own once that was announced, taking them off the hook for the layoffs that were probably already in the works. We tried to joke about it. You know, 'Another day, another 85 cents.' "

Other cuts may accompany a company's sudden cost-consciousness. Travel budgets may be reduced or eliminated. The company may decide to reduce or eliminate such benefits as employee training. Sometimes the cost cuts are petty and desperate, as when the company decides to eliminate free coffee for employees. In any case, a string of cost-cutting measures may be followed by the more severe measure of general layoffs.

You need to remember that a company desperate enough to start taking money out of its employees' paychecks is likely to be on the verge of more severe actions. This warning sign may be one of the most important. Remember, if they lay you off *after* the pay cut, you'll receive that much less severance pay during a time when you'll really need it.

Widespread Early Retirement

Again, before resorting to layoffs a company may try a number of cost-cutting measures. If the company has a large number of employees who have significant tenure and are near retirement age, the company may try to entice them to retire early. The logic of this approach is based on the fact that these people have the highest salaries. The company can actually save money by enticing them to retire if it means that those high salaries are off the payroll.

Many large companies have tried this approach and then later had to resort to layoffs. Digital Equipment Corp. and AT&T once operated under a "no layoff" policy. After offering voluntary layoffs and early retirements, both eventually had to employ general layoffs to reduce head count.

Whew, I Survived

One more note: Just because you survived a layoff with your job intact, don't assume you are safe. One of the key early warning signs of an impending layoff may be a layoff itself. Often when one layoff fails to produce needed cost savings, a second or third will follow. Sensible companies choose to lay off as many people as necessary quickly, to allow the remaining people to get on with the business of rebuilding what's left of the company. The "do it quickly and get it over with" philosophy doesn't always prevail, however. Some companies will try to lose a few employees at a time in the hopes of keeping all they can possibly afford to keep. Once a company starts laying off employees, you should generally assume you are not safe until significant evidence to the contrary presents itself.

"Luckily," Frank said, "the company got a little smarter after the first couple of layoffs they went through. In the earlier years, they knew they had to keep good talent to get the company off the ground. So they'd try to let just one or two people go. The result was that one or two weeks later they'd have to cut someone else. I felt relieved after the first two people were laid off that first time. After that, I learned never to trust them until the sales numbers started moving up again."

BEING PREPARED

Suppose the early warning signs are evident, and you fear your job may be on the line. What do you do next? First, and most important, regardless of how important you believe you are to the company, always prepare for the worst and assume you are on the list. This allows you to do three things: accelerate your search for a new position, proactively provide a case to support your current value to the company in hopes of keeping your job or, if you're unsuccessful with the first two ideas, you can prepare for a departure that offers you the most security possible.

Should You Jump Ship?

If your company is in trouble and management is trying to maintain reasonable control, this is a question they may not want you to be considering. Regardless of the company's concerns, however, you need to consider your own future and your family's well-being. There are many factors that enter into your decision about whether or not to leave your current employer. A few important ones to consider are:

Do you have a reasonable alternative? If you have other employment possibilities, you need to weigh a number of factors about those possibilities. How much will you earn? Will it advance your career or stall it? Will a new job require some sacrifice from you or your family?

How does your company handle layoffs? If your company doesn't have a history of laying people off, you may not be able to answer this question. However, if your company generally provides generous severance packages, you may feel that it's worth the financial risk to stay with them and ride out the storm. If the company is notoriously cheap, however, you may not want to wait.

What are the prospects for recovery? Is the company's current situation temporary? The company may have some positive steps in the works to quickly turn around its fortunes. On the other hand, the company may be trying to sell buggy whips, all the while not realizing that the market for buggy whips died long ago.

Although it sounds callous, as you make your decision to leave you must absolutely disregard any feelings of loyalty to the company. Almost to a person, individuals who are laid off will tell you that they couldn't believe they'd been let go, considering how loyal they'd been to the company. The overwhelming response of people who have been laid off is that they regret having put their loyalty to the company ahead of their concern for the financial security of their own family. When you consider the question in that light, you may reach a conclusion very quickly.

Making Your Case

You may decide not to leave the company or you may not have an appropriate alternative position when you need one. At this point, if you believe the company is in trouble and have reason to believe layoffs are imminent, don't assume that your years of service, exceptional performance, or loyalty to the company will be enough to save your job. The committee currently evaluating who stays and who goes may be looking at bottom-line criteria that may have little to do with your intrinsic value to the company. Most companies will try to keep employees they don't believe can be easily replaced. However, if your salary is significantly higher than those of your peers or you are more talented and capable than your boss, your name may be on the list. You need to develop a case highlighting your value to the company and present the case, reasonably and calmly, to the highest-level decision maker you can approach.

Your case should present immediate, bottom-line benefits to the company if they choose to keep you. For example, you can present a plan to ensure completion of a key project while eliminating contract or temporary employees currently assigned to the project. You may be able to show that you can cut your travel budget by one-half or two-thirds and still promise to meet sales quotas. In short, the more financially attractive you can make your case, the more impact it will have.

Presenting your case can be a delicate issue, especially if no official announcements about layoffs have yet been released. You can choose the up-front approach and tell company management that you understand the company is having financial difficulties and that, in the interest of staying with the company and helping it become more successful, you'd like to present your capabilities and a plan to help ease the company's financial burden. This direct approach shows inventiveness on your part and provides a positive message, quite possibly the only good news your management hears during a difficult time.

As mentioned earlier, if your company has already had one or more "everything's okay" meetings, the door is open for you to discuss the situation more directly with your manager. In some cases, by showing concern for the company's financial situation, you may make it easier for your manager to give you information that can help you. If you are currently considered too valuable to lose, your showing of concern may allow your manager to relieve your fears and tell you that your job is not on the line.

A less direct approach may be necessary if you think overtly mentioning the company's financial problems is not a good idea. Simply providing an innovative, unsolicited way to cut costs or increase revenues to your department or company will increase your value to the company and possibly keep your name off the list.

One note of caution: No matter how much you need your current job, asking to be spared a layoff or downright pleading to be saved are bad ideas. Not only do they not show your managers any reason to save your position, they also create an extremely difficult working environment for you and your manager. Pleading for a co-worker's position will have similar effects.

Preparing for the Inevitable

"The manager of our editing group asked me to come into her office and bring the article I was working on," Marlene said. "It wasn't an odd request, and I didn't expect anything unusual. When I sat down, she closed the door and said, 'I'm sorry to have to be the one to tell you this, but the company has decided to lay you off.'

"She went on talking about revenues and how exceptional my work was and that she'd write me a great reference letter, but I didn't hear any of it. My heart was pounding and I felt I was choking. I remember seeing the pages of my article on the floor, and I wondered if I should pick them up. My boss was saying something about two weeks' notice when I left the room, went to my office, and sobbed for fifteen minutes."

In some situations, you may not have a chance to make your case. Even if you have been watching for the early warning signs of a layoff, sudden, sweeping announcements may preclude any discussion. On the other hand, even if you present a clear and coherent argument, it may not have its desired effect. If the company is desperate enough, they may even use your ideas *and* lay you off. In any event, you should be prepared for the worst.

Chapters 3 and 6 provide advice for someone who has recently been laid off. They are also good advice if you *anticipate* a layoff. It is most important for you to think clearly and plan ahead so that you negotiate the best situation you can to provide your family the most security possible.

When interviewed after a sudden layoff, most people say that their first reaction upon hearing the news was shock, followed by disbelief, anger, confusion, or any of a host of disabling emotions that make it difficult to navigate one of the most treacherous business situations. By carefully reviewing your family's financial situation and carefully planning what you think you can reasonably get in terms of a severance arrangement, you will be better able to deal with the situation.

If you can, role play a layoff scenario with someone you trust. Just hearing the words, "I'm sorry, we're going to have to let you go," spoken out loud will be enough to jolt your consciousness into action. Take the role-play seriously and imagine your boss actually telling you you're about to lose your job. The role-playing experience may be uncomfortable, but it will allow you to be sure of how you will react.

One other important note on preparation: If you think you are about to be laid off, find out everything you can about your company's attitudes toward and past arrangements for severance agreements. Most companies provide some sort of severance pay for laid-off employees. As you will find out in Chapter 2, what you receive may depend entirely on your ability to negotiate for it. In that respect, you need to know what has been done in the past to ascertain what the company considers fair and equitable. Talk to fellow employees who may have survived previous layoffs. Talk to people who have been laid off previously. Find out all you can about what to expect. This will help you get the best arrangement you possibly can.

Other Details

After being laid off, most people think of at least a handful of things they wish they had done immediately before their layoff. For one reason or another, you may find it impossible to complete some of these important tasks once you have been asked to leave.

If you're concerned about your current situation, do several things now:

Make sure you have your network in place. As any good employment counselor will tell you, most new jobs are found through the network of contacts you build over time. Before you are asked to leave, make sure you have copies of all the important addresses and telephone numbers you will need. Take your business card file or telephone card file home and copy down every name, address, and telephone number. Your company may choose to keep these items after you have left, leaving you without critical information with which to begin your new search.

Take a close look at your financial picture. Use the ideas presented in Chapter 6 to get a clear understanding of your financial picture. If you don't think you can survive for 9 to 12 months on your current savings, you might want to consider a home equity loan or other type of low-interest loan. It will be much easier to receive approval for such a loan while you still have a job than it will be if you are laid off.

Find out how many vacation and personal days you have left. In the event you are laid off, most companies will pay you for vacation days you have earned but not used. The same may not be true for personal days or floating holidays, however. Talk to a human resources representative to determine what days you have available. In general, you should not use any available vacation days, because the pay you receive for them will be helpful if you are laid off. Personal days or floating holidays for which you may not receive pay should be used judiciously. You may already be interviewing or you may choose to take a day to research potential job leads.

Use any other benefits. If you haven't had a checkup in a while, schedule one right away, and go to the dentist. If you need a physical or other medical exam, do it now. You may lose your medical and dental benefits immediately after you leave or after your severance agreement ends. With the staggering cost of medical care in recent years, you are better off to let your current insurance provider pay while you still have the option.

Remove personal files. After you are laid off, there may be a question as to what belongs to you and what belongs to the company. In fact, you may not even have access to your office in the event you are laid off. To be on the safe side, remove personal files such as insurance or benefits records. Do not, however, take anything that belongs to the company or is of a proprietary nature.

2 | The Day You Find Out

Jim was a project manager for a software company.

"When he told me he was laying me off," Jim said, "I actually laughed at him. I honestly thought he was joking. When he didn't say anything after that, it started to sink in. He was *serious*. After six straight weeks of overtime hours and working on weekends, this department head was standing there in the lab telling me I was out of a job. I wanted to deck him, and I almost did. Instead I shoved my chair back from the desk and pushed my keyboard away from me. It crashed when it hit the floor, and several keys popped off and went flying. My boss stood back and looked scared. I think *he* thought I was going to deck him."

If you never have to experience a layoff, you are spared one of the most painful and difficult situations anyone has to face. Layoffs are personally devastating and financially difficult. A layoff can alienate you from former co-workers and friends and damage professional relationships you have worked hard to develop. Advance planning, however, can make your exit as positive as possible for everyone involved, thereby salvaging your reputation and some professional relationships that may be valuable to you in the future. This chapter deals with how to react when you are faced with the news that you will be laid off, and how to maintain positive relationships with former co-workers.

THE INDIGNITY OF IT ALL

Depending on how prepared you are for the news that your job is being eliminated, your reactions will span a complete range of emotions. If you are not prepared, you will be stunned that they could possibly think of letting *you* go, furious that your loyalty and service to the company were not considered, and certainly angry that they could do this to you.

If you are prepared (as briefly discussed in Chapter 1), you will still feel all these responses, but you will be better able to handle the situation and get what you need out of it. The most important thing to remember is that, by being laid off, you are suddenly thrust into an important business situation in which you need to have a clear head to negotiate effectively for what you need. In that respect, you must find a way to retain control of your emotions and reactions and deal with your (now former) employers in a logical manner. In short, to borrow from a well-known deodorant commercial, "Never let 'em see you sweat."

When you receive the news, no matter how much you'd like to scream, cry, throw things, hurt someone, or generally explode, don't do it. Or at least don't do it in front of the people laying you off. Don't make threats of any kind. Don't say anything that will harm you and your bargaining position. (For more information on why this is critical, see "Severance Pay," later in this chapter.) If you feel the need to react emotionally in any way, take a deep breath, calmly excuse yourself, and go to a private place (preferably with a door you can close) and cool off. If you have a friend or person you know you can lean on at this point, quietly ask him or her to spend a few minutes with you.

There is one very critical thing to remember when you get the news: You must be prepared to negotiate; strong emotions will put you at a disadvantage. The moment you receive the news, if you are not prepared to negotiate calmly, *leave the room*. The people firing you may not appreciate your walking out on the discussion, but that, frankly, is their problem. You have every right to deal with this difficult situation in a way that protects you and your reputation.

SEVERANCE PAY: NEGOTIATING AN EQUITABLE OFFER

According to Judith Dowdle and Stephen Eide, two attorneys who specialize in employee benefits, "The HR manager's natural inclination is to keep severance-pay policies hidden from view. Workers may not be able to find details on severance pay in the employee manual, even though severance pay is often a significant benefit. Instead, such policies exist only as confidential notes tucked away in a file drawer. By avoiding a policy set in stone, the HR manager hopes to remain free to deal with each severance-pay situation individually."

In an article in *Personnel* magazine, Dowdle and Eide go on to say that most companies do not publish any printed information on severance policies. Companies do this to allow company management to deal with each severance arrangement as an individual negotiation. In fact, a survey by the Administrative Management Society showed that approximately 60 percent of the companies the society surveyed had no formal severance policy.

This evidence should lead you to believe that, no matter what your former manager tells you, there is no such thing as a "standard" severance arrangement. The more research you have done about your company's past performance in this area (see

"Being Prepared" in Chapter 1), the better your chances will be of getting what you need.

Some companies use a formula (based on such factors as seniority or job title) to determine your severance agreement. But, as when companies hire new employees, these "formulas" are often only a starting point. If you are skeptical on this point, ask yourself if you believe that everyone at your level with approximately your experience is currently paid the exact same salary by your company. The answer is certainly no. When you are hired, you negotiate a salary that may be significantly higher than those of your peers, for no other reason than the fact that you are a better negotiator than they were when they were hired. The same holds true for negotiating severance pay.

Some Standards

To give you an idea of an average severance arrangement, *American Demographics* magazine quotes figures compiled by Drake Beam Morin, a New York outplacement firm. In 1988 the firm dealt with a variety of clients in all age groups, with an average age of 44. Drake Beam Morin's clients tend to come from middle-management positions with several years of professional experience. Still, the average length of severance pay for these professionals was 6.7 months.

You should also know that, under the law, severance-pay programs are covered under the Employee Retirement Income Security Act (ERISA), making such plans subject to government regulation. Again, companies may tend to be secretive about past severance agreements because, under the ERISA, employees can sue if they feel they are not receiving adequate severance compensation. An attorney will be able to provide more information on the ERISA, should you need to use it to appeal your company's severance offer. (See "How to Appeal" later in this chapter.)

What to Ask For

When the company hired you, you negotiated a starting salary. As with a starting salary, there is no set formula to use when determining what you should ask for in a severance arrangement. In general, the more you know about past arrangements, the better prepared you will be to state your case. Before any discussion of severance pay is begun, be sure of what you expect, and be ready to ask for it. Some things to consider are listed as follows:

> *Term of the agreement and payments.* Not only is it important to discuss the term of the agreement, you should also be prepared to discuss the nature and timing of severance payments. Will you continue "on the payroll" or will you simply receive a lump-sum payment? Before you decide, you might want to call your local unemployment office to determine how such payments can affect your eligibility for unemployment insurance. (See Chapter 5, "The Unemployment Office.") In addition, your decision about whether to stay on the payroll can hinge on your current eligibility for your company's pension plan. While you remain on the payroll, the company will continue to make contributions.

> *Extension of benefits.* Medical and dental bills can pile up quickly, especially if you have a family. Providing you with continued coverage throughout the severance period is not a large cost to the company. The lack of such coverage can, however, be a huge cost to you. Disability insurance is another benefit the company pays for that you may not be able to do without. Although the odds of your having a disabling accident during a period of unemployment are small, you still need to protect yourself from financial disaster. The issue of benefits is an important bargaining chip in your severance negotiations.

If you cannot get your employer to extend your benefits at no cost to you, you should be aware that under the law your employer may be required to allow you to buy insurance at the company's group rate for a certain period of time after your position is terminated. According to a statute of the Consolidated Omnibus Budget Reconciliation Act (COBRA) of 1986, your employer may be required to allow you to participate in the company's group health plan for up to 18 months from the date of your termination. A few criteria may apply, but in general, if your employer has more than 20 employees and you were not terminated for misconduct, you should be eligible to continue to receive health benefits for which you pay the group rate. Your employer's human resources manager should have information on COBRA laws and their impact on your situation.

Assistance in finding a new job. Don't ever underestimate the difficulty of finding a new job. Even if you believe you have a new one in the bag, offers can fall through. Ask for and use whatever resources the company may have available. If the company uses an outplacement firm for hiring, ask to use the firm to aid you in your search. Access to computers, printers, secretarial assistance, and any other support will come in handy as you look for a new position.

Counseling support and services. Job loss will have a significant impact on you and your family. Your company may provide counseling services free of charge for dealing with the emotional and financial aspects of losing your job.

Other benefits. If you drive a company car, ask to keep it while under the severance agreement. While you are unemployed, the last thing you need to do is shop for a new car. If you can hang on to any other miscellaneous benefits (computer hardware you've been using at home, for example), it can help.

Cancellation of the agreement. Some employers offer severance pay only until you find another position or until the severance term expires, whichever comes first. You should be clear on this point. Severance pay is a benefit due you, regardless of what happens after you leave the company. If you are especially effective in your job search, you should not be penalized by your former employer for finding a new position quickly. After all, they won't extend your severance period if you don't find a job before it expires. Why should you forfeit money you've earned simply because you're tenacious about finding a new job?

You may find it difficult to think in terms of negotiating for severance pay. Again, because most companies do not publish severance policies, you may not know where to begin. Dr. Laurence Stybel, president of Stybel, Peabody & Associates of Boston, empathizes with people who are suddenly thrown into negotiations for a severance agreement. He explains, "Negotiating a severance arrangement with someone who has just fired you may feel like playing poker with an opponent who has a royal flush—and you have no cards." Dr. Stybel goes on to say, "Yet, you may be in a more favorable position than you think if you know when to negotiate, what to negotiate, and with whom."

Make the First Move

As soon as you are able after you have been notified of your termination, you should be the one to bring up severance pay. By being the first to bring it up, you let your employer know that you assume you will receive a severance agreement and that you have very definite ideas on what the arrangement should be. Your opening offer should be direct and certain: "I understand that my termination is a necessary decision given the company's financial situation. From past experience, you have dealt fairly with other employees who have been laid off. Because of that, I am confident that my severance package will be at least the following: (give your plan for the severance arrangement)."

Remember to include all important items: State the amount of severance pay you expect and how long you expect your benefits to be continued. In addition, if your company gives outstanding vacation pay to employees who voluntarily leave the company, you should reasonably expect to receive payment for outstanding vacation days *in addition to* any severance pay. As when you negotiated a starting salary, know what you need, be prepared to ask for everything, and know what you can give up.

Know Your Bargaining Chips

When negotiating a severance agreement, you obviously don't have the leverage you had when you negotiated a starting salary with the company. After all, then they wanted to hire you; now they want to lay you off. If they don't agree to give you what you ask for, you certainly can't threaten not to work for them! However, you will have three things in your favor: an element of surprise, an appeal to fairness, and a rudimentary knowledge of laws governing severance arrangements.

The element of surprise lies in the fact that most people, upon hearing that they are being laid off, are too shocked to negotiate a severance agreement. Jane Ciabattari, a contributing editor for *Working Woman* magazine, says, "Some companies will offer you a severance package amounting to two weeks' salary and send you out the door fast, while you're still in shock." If you are calmly prepared and approach the subject firmly, in most cases your employer will be somewhat surprised if not downright dumbfounded. After all, the last thing they expect is a cool-headed negotiator. If you can muster the courage needed to handle the situation firmly, you will have an advantage.

The second element in your favor lies in the fact that nearly anyone, no matter how callous, would have difficulty laying off an employee, especially one who has been valuable to the organization. In fact, the person giving you the news may feel completely miserable about the prospect. If you are firm in your demands and can tactfully appeal to his or her sense of fairness, you will have an advantage. A manager with any empathy at all will find it difficult enough to tell you you're out of a job. Putting the screws to you on a severance agreement will likely be more than he or she can stomach, especially if you are calm and persistent.

The third element in your favor rests on the fact that severance agreements are covered by federal law. In other words, companies cannot be capricious in their approach to severance packages. You don't have to threaten to sue, but you can mention that you know that under federal law you are entitled to reasonably fair treatment when it comes to severance pay. The fact that you're knowledgeable in this area will likely throw a manager off guard, because most managers will be ignorant of the laws governing severance pay. If your manager is more concerned about the company's overall liability than about giving you an extra month or two, you have scored an important negotiating point.

How to Appeal

What if it doesn't work? What if you appeal to their fairness, firmly present a reasonable severance package, and discuss the issue until you're blue in the face—and the company still will not capitulate? "Two weeks is all you're getting. Period." You do have options. In fact, as mentioned earlier in this chapter, the law is generally on your side. However, if you mention this fact to your (now previous) employer, mention that you have an idea of what others have received, and that if they still don't see it your way, you may have to resort to other means.

If your employer is stubborn, cheap, or ignorant of the law, you may need to discuss your options with an attorney. Suing an employer should always be your *last* option; a well-timed letter from an attorney, however, can be all a company needs to begin to see your side of the bargain. As soon as the company begins adding up potential bills from attorneys, they'll soon realize that even doubling or tripling your severance package is a bargain in comparison.

One note: If your employer treats you fairly, don't try to use an attorney simply to wring more money out of him or her. Not only will you not have a leg to stand on under the law, you may also spend too much of your own funds chasing something that can add very little value to your current situation. Again, legal counsel should be your last recourse and should be used only when you are reasonably sure the return on your investment will justify the expense.

Get It in Writing

Depending on your situation, your employer may be purposely vague about your severance arrangement. "Because of our financial situation, we can't afford to keep you on permanently. But you just go ahead and take as much time as you need to find something new. We'll relieve you of your responsibilities so you can use your time here to find another position." Statements like these may sound comforting and reassuring, but they put your employer in control. What happens when you've been looking for three months and haven't found anything? Will your employer's patience wear thin, along with your severance pay?

Regardless of your relationship with your employer, you must get everything in writing. Make a point of agreeing on every detail, put it in writing, and sign it after getting your employer to sign it.

One important note about getting it in writing: Although it

may seem like a trivial detail, be sure that your written agreement includes the actual amount you will be paid and over what period. Your employer may agree to keep you "on the payroll" for several weeks or months. However, if your employer continues to have financial problems and considers across-the-board pay cuts, he or she may feel justified in cutting your severance pay as well. Be sure your severance agreement states that your severance pay will be based on *your current salary*.

Finally, be sure the written agreement clearly states why you are being let go. Assuming you are not being fired for some sort of gross misconduct, make sure your employer signs a paper stating that you are being laid off for financial reasons, because of a personality conflict, or because your skills no longer fit the company's needs. Most likely no one but you will ever see this document, but the wording of your employer's reasons for letting you go can have an impact on your unemployment compensation benefits. For more information on why this is important, see "Appealing a Bad Decision" in Chapter 5.

TO RETURN OR NOT TO RETURN

You have one more decision to make as you negotiate your departure: Is there a possibility the company could hire you back and, if so, do you want to come back? Many people are too angry and upset to even consider this question. In fact, your first response to the question may be "No way in hell." However, as with the severance pay issue, the question is one that should be evaluated and answered logically, focusing on your current financial situation, the current economic outlook in your area, and your specific marketable skills.

In any event, if you handle yourself calmly and professionally throughout the process of being notified and negotiating your severance agreement, you will be able to leave the door open to return. You may even wish to approach the subject before you leave the company. Let your employer know that you value the experience you gained with the company, that you believe in their ability to turn the company around financially, and that you'd like to be considered when the company begins to grow again.

LEAVING ON A POSITIVE NOTE

Regardless of how you feel about the company, your manager, and the whole situation of being let go, you should make every effort to leave on a positive note. Take a minute to talk with co-workers, particularly those with whom you've enjoyed working. Again, be sure you are calm enough to do this in a positive way. Under no circumstances should you denigrate the company or its management. At this point, it's best to stick to your mother's old adage, "If you don't have anything nice to say, don't say anything at all."

As you look for a new position and continue on in your career, the contacts you have made in the past will always be valuable to you. No matter how angry you are at being laid off, don't burn bridges. If you feel too upset to talk with anyone, leave and come back later, or call each individual to tell him or her how much you've appreciated the chance to work with him or her. The reputation you save will be your own.

WHAT TO TELL YOUR CLIENTS OR CUSTOMERS

If you are in sales, marketing, customer support, or any one of a number of areas that requires direct customer contact, you and your employer will ponder the question of what to tell your clients. If your company is large and the layoffs are public knowledge, your employer will feel reasonably comfortable if you choose to call your customers and tell them the situation. If you are departing from the company because of unfulfilled promises or other friction between you and the company's management, you may wish to tell your customers nothing more than that you are resigning under duress and that you'd rather not go into a great deal of detail about the situation.

If your departure is a result of financial difficulties that are not well known, the problem is somewhat more difficult. You and your employer may have opposing viewpoints on what to tell customers. Your employer wants to maintain the company's reputation and keep valuable customers from finding some other supplier because they become concerned over the company's financial state. On the other hand, you have your own reputation to protect. Allowing your employer to tell customers anything but the truth can damage your reputation. The best approach is to discuss the question openly and honestly with your employer. Tell him or her that you plan to call each of your valued customers to inform them that you will be leaving the company. You can reinforce to the customer that you have every confidence in the company and that you hope to stay in touch with him or her.

Again, the most important thing to remember is to be positive. You personally gain nothing by dragging your employer's name through the mud, regardless of how angry you are that your job has been terminated. The best approach is to be as positive as possible and retain all important business contacts. This strategy will protect your reputation, ensure a positive departure from your company, and possibly even provide you with a valuable source of job leads.

One note: Under no circumstances should you allow your employer to sacrifice you to save his or her own reputation. Don't let your employer tell the customer that you quit on your own, were fired for cause, or took another position, unless, of course, any of those things actually happened.

3 | The Emotional Impact

Lynn was a project manager for an industrial design firm. She remembers the day she was laid off: "There was no doubt the company was in trouble. We'd watched as they tried everything to keep it afloat: vacations without pay, early retirements, you name it. Whenever I talked about it with my husband, though, I always talked about how worried I was about some of the young people working for me. How would their families survive? I remember the day they told me. I drove home in this state of shock wondering, 'How am I going to tell Paul and the kids?' When I got home I didn't have to say anything. I burst into tears as I walked through the door. That's how they knew. I *never* thought it would be me. How could they do this to me? Didn't they understand how important I was to the operation? That's when it hit me: I guess I just wasn't as important as I thought I was. Maybe I really wasn't all that good."

Few experiences in life are more devastating than sitting in a room listening to someone tell you that you are out of a job. No matter how they say it, the news hits you like a fist in the stomach. Your heart pounds, your mind races, you aren't sure if you should cry or hit someone. You put a few things in a cardboard box (or someone has already done it for you) and drive home dazed.

The anger and betrayal are soon replaced by panic as you wonder how you'll make the mortgage payments. In fact, that is what makes job loss so difficult: At a time when you are already dealing with a huge psychological blow, you are suddenly thrust into the middle of a potentially severe financial crisis. You now have not just *one* problem, you have two. Not only do you have to somehow survive the personal devastation of losing a job, you also have to manage on one less income.

Add a spouse and one or more children depending on you and the emotional distress can seem overwhelming. There may not seem to be much good news when you find out you've lost a job. The most important thing to remember if it happens to you is: You are not alone. Despite the anger, depression, and isolation you may feel, there are hundreds of thousands of competent, hard-working, talented people who have lost jobs. Some experts estimate that as many as two out of three people will be fired or laid off at one time during their careers. You aren't the first, and you can learn from their experiences. This chapter recounts some of the experiences of people who have survived exactly what you sometimes feel you cannot survive. In their stories, and in the strategies they used to survive the emotional impact of losing a job, you can find ways to work through one of the most difficult times in your life.

ON A SCALE OF ONE TO TEN, I'D GIVE IT A FORTY-SEVEN

There is no doubt that job loss is one of the most stressful situations anyone can endure. As you face the turbulent emotions, it may help you to understand what is happening to you and to know what to expect. In an effort to measure the impact of major stresses on people's lives, Dr. Thomas Holmes of the University of Washington School of Medicine developed what he calls the social readjustment rating scale. This scale numerically rates life events associated with varying amounts of disruption on the average person's life. The higher the rating, the more stressful the event. Here are a few of the major stress events and their ratings:

Event	Numerical Impact
Death of a spouse	100
Divorce	73
Marital separation	65
Jail term	63
Death of a close family member	63
Personal injury or illness	53
Marriage	50
Fired at work	47
Retirement	45
Pregnancy	40
Change in health of a family member	39
Business readjustment	39

As you can see, losing your job is not quite as bad as going to jail but certainly worse than being pregnant. The point is, you are *supposed* to feel lousy. Losing your job is a terrible insult to your self-esteem, no matter what the situation was that put you out of work. What you are feeling is grief for a terrible loss you have experienced. Your emotions as a response to this loss will range from anger and betrayal to disappointment and hurt. If you know what to expect, you can be better prepared to deal with the impact on your life.

SELF-ESTEEM AND JOB LOSS

No matter what your company was going through at the time they let you go, unless they closed down altogether you can't help thinking, "Why me? Why not someone else?" One of the most difficult aspects of job loss is that most people's initial reaction is that they somehow deserved it: Did I disagree with my manager once too often? Did I project the wrong budget numbers? Did I offend someone in some way? The almost universal response to job loss is that it has to be the fault of the person being laid off.

Lynn remembers missing a dinner party hosted by her boss just before she was laid off. "I kept thinking, 'Maybe I should have gone to his party. Maybe *that* was my big mistake.' His family had just built a lake-front house and I think they wanted to show it off. I guess I should have gone to the party."

The important thing to remember when you start to believe you caused the situation is that there is a difference between taking responsibility and blaming yourself. There may be some things you would do differently if given the chance, but you have to realize that in all likelihood you would still be out of a job. Especially during difficult economic times, job loss is most likely due to economic concerns rather than personal differences. In fact, even if you *were* let go because of a "personality conflict," instead of berating yourself for past mistakes, take responsibility for learning what you can that will help you move forward in your career.

Insensitivity and Anger

One of the more difficult emotional aspects of losing your job often stems from the way most companies handle terminations. Many companies are clumsy or downright inept in the way they conduct layoffs. Their rough treatment of you can further exacerbate the feeling that you somehow brought it on yourself. If your employer handled the situation badly, you need to remember that it likely had nothing to do with you and your performance. Layoff horror stories abound. Some of the better ones are:

> A large defense contractor had several sales offices across the country. When the decision was made to close many of these offices, the company flew all affected employees to the company's California headquarters for an important company meeting. On a Sunday night, far away from family and friends, these people were told they were out of a job. Many of them were given only two weeks' severance pay. "What could we do at this point?" one woman asked. "Everybody headed straight for the hotel bar to start drinking."

> A young broker for a Chicago brokerage firm found out he was out of work when he received a certified letter on a Saturday morning informing him that his company was dropping his insurance coverage.

> A brand manager for a consumer products firm had a stellar annual review and received the highest possible raise for someone at her management level. Three weeks later her boss called her in to tell her she was losing her job and that she should clean out her office "within the hour."

When faced with the prospect of having to fire someone, most managers react badly. In addition, most companies believe that an abrupt, terse termination is the best approach when laying off employees. The result is usually an insensitive or even cruel experience for the person being laid off.

Lynn remembers thinking, "The hardest thing for me was the way they dealt with me. I had put heart and soul into that company. I'd worked overtime whenever they needed it. I really *cared* about my work and the designers who worked for me. I never dealt with the company in a 'bottom-line' way. It really hurt that they saw me as just one extra salary to do away with. They certainly used bottom-line criteria when they let me go."

In addition to the clumsy handling of employee terminations, many companies inflict more damage trying to justify their actions afterwards. If you maintain contact with some of the people left behind, you may find that the real reasons for the company's actions take on a different light. In an effort to bolster the sagging morale of remaining employees, your former employer may try to make it seem as if the people who were laid off were somehow at fault.

"I remember talking to one of the other accountants in the department not long after I was laid off," one woman recalls. "He told me a rumor had started that I wasn't laid off after all. One of the bookkeepers had said to him, 'Oh, come on, Phil, don't you realize that she wasn't laid off, she was *fired*?' There was no effort on my former manager's part to stop any of the rumors. I remember how sick it made me feel that people I used to work with were wondering what I did to get fired."

Rumors about the "real" reasons behind termination tend to move quickly within a company. Your former manager may do little to stop such rumors because it takes the heat off him or her for letting you go. In addition, many people left behind will cling to such rumors because it offers them a way to justify what happened. If they believe your termination was a random event caused by the company's financial problems, that means they could be next. If, on the other hand, they believe you did something awful to get fired, the people left behind can sleep better at night.

Unfounded rumors about your performance are usually more damaging to your self-esteem than to your career. Rather than dwell on the situation, you need to ignore people's often petty need to distort the issues behind sudden layoffs. As you concentrate on finding a new position, realize that the unfounded opinions of former co-workers are not relevant to your future and can only hinder your progress if you dwell on them.

It's Not as Embarrassing as You Think

"The first few days I was home, I didn't know where to start," one unemployed editor recalls. "My wife suggested that I call some friends and colleagues for help and advice. I told her, 'No need. I have my own ideas.' In truth, I was too embarrassed to tell *anyone* I was out of work. I didn't want to see any of our friends, and I avoided situations that meant I'd have to see them. I refused to go to any social gatherings. One day I realized I hadn't even been outside the house in more than ten days."

If someone steals your car, if a close friend or family member dies, or if your house is decimated by a tornado, you wouldn't think to react with embarrassment and shame. In some ways, job loss can be just as random an event as any of those tragedies, yet many people still feel humiliation, refusing to ask for help and support while looking for a new job.

"I realized I'd been hiding for two months," one business analyst said of her six-month period of unemployment. "I hadn't even told my own *parents* that I was out of work. It was as if I had been caught driving under the influence or something. As I look back on that now, I realize how self-defeating it was not to start talking to people right away. All the job experts tell you to network. How could I network in my family room with the blinds drawn and my answering machine on?"

Of all the emotional reactions to losing a job, shame and embarrassment can be the most damaging. If you are too embarrassed to talk to people, your most valuable job-search tool —networking—is destroyed. One of the best ways to combat feelings of embarrassment over losing your job is to talk with others who have suffered the same fate. Commiserate with someone who was laid off with you, even if you don't know the person very well. Find out if a local church or community organization has a support group for people who have experienced sudden job loss. Above all, do it quickly. Because embarrassment over losing your job is counterproductive, you need to disarm the feeling before it can sidetrack your critical job-search tasks.

Dealing with All Those Stupid Comments

"People's reactions when I told them I was laid off reminded me of some of the dumb things people say at funerals," one un-employed job-seeker recalls. "Let's face it, people don't deal with crises very well. Sometimes they say some of the most inane things. If I didn't need their help as I looked for a new job, I would have avoided them altogether."

As you start to explain your recent job loss to people, you may find that they react with clumsy or insensitive comments. Your mother-in-law suggests that this is a sign that you should really stay home and have children. Your neighbor asks what you did to get fired. Your friend tells you about someone she knew who was out of work for *three years* and lost every possession he owned.

Many people don't deal well with bad news. You shouldn't let this deter you from using all the contacts you have as you look for a new job. Remember that people can be uncomfortable with the situation. Like a sudden death, a friend's or relative's job loss can hit close to home for some people. Their first re-actions may be inappropriate and ineffective. Don't let such awk-ward reactions stop you from talking to people in your network who can be critical to your job search.

OPEN-ENDED ANXIETY

Day one. Day ten. Day thirty. "What if I never find another job?" Unemployment creates an open-ended situation from which you cannot escape until you find another job. Because you have no idea when that will be, your anxiety can grow with each passing day. Left unchecked, anxiety can paralyze you and frustrate your job search.

Rather than let the anxiety grow into panic, you need to find ways to be in control. If you suddenly find yourself out of work, two key areas will seem calamitous, finances and your job search. The two are obviously linked: The longer it takes you to find another job, the more serious your financial situation will become. Chapters 6 and 8 give a concrete prescription for managing your financial situation and beginning your job search.

Before you let your anxiety get the best of you, read both chapters and define your own concrete plan for managing these critical areas. Create a complete budget plan. Get out a calendar and give yourself deadlines for creating your network list, designing a resumé, and making a set number of telephone calls. In short, give yourself a job. If you realize that finding a new job will take some time but that you have control of your finances and your job search plans, you can drastically reduce the effects of open-ended anxiety.

Once again, the point is to act quickly to disarm the fears that can damage your job-search prospects. Don't spend three days worrying about finances before ever digging out your bank statements and putting a budget on paper. The sooner you start working on solving your unemployment problem, the more in control you will feel.

DEPRESSION

Phil is a construction supervisor who has been through several layoffs. "The first time," he recalls, "I had a simple solution to the problem: I drank. A lot. I'm not sure if I drank because I was depressed or if I was depressed because I drank, but I've learned since then never to do that again."

Many psychologists believe that reactions to sudden job loss are very much like the reactions people have to divorce or the death of a loved one: first shock, then anger and grief, and, finally, acceptance of the inevitable. Because anger and grief are a nearly unavoidable part of the emotional reaction to losing a job, depression can easily follow.

If you have struggled with bouts of depression in the past, you may be especially susceptible. Even if you have not experienced depression before, you should be on the lookout for some important warning signs, including:

■ gloomy feelings of sadness

■ feelings of helplessness

■ increasingly negative or hopeless thoughts

■ withdrawal from other people

■ lack of motivation/inability to start or complete activities

■ loss of concentration

■ difficulty falling asleep

■ waking early yet still feeling fatigued

■ loss of appetite

Depressed people tend to withdraw more and more from others. Feelings of hopelessness can be suffocating at times. You may find it hard to concentrate on tasks such as revising your resume. You may feel fatigued even though you spend much more time in bed and find it difficult to get up in the morning. Depression is a common reaction to loss of any kind and it can be debilitating.

There are a number of simple things you can do to counteract the effects of mild depression. Within reasonable limits, allow yourself to get more rest. You shouldn't stay in bed all day, but an hour or two of extra sleep can help you recover from the shock you have received. Exercise can be the best way to counteract the effects of depression. As long as you are in reasonably good physical health, spend at least one half-hour each day doing some kind of vigorous exercise. Swim, ride a stationary bike, find an aerobics program on public television. If you are not in good physical condition, you will need to start slowly. A good 20-minute walk can help get your blood circulating enough to make you feel better.

To ward off the effects of depression, you should be careful about what you eat and drink. Eat a balanced diet, and stay away from alcohol and caffeine. Alcohol is a depressant that may make you feel better temporarily but will almost certainly aggravate your emotional response to being out of work. Caffeine can perk you up momentarily, but it can also affect your ability to sleep well and feel rested.

GETTING HELP

By all means, if you start to feel overwhelmed by depression or anxiety, do not hesitate to get professional help. If you even have *one* suicidal thought, if you start to think your family would be better with the insurance money than with you around, *get help at once*. Find a competent professional with whom you can discuss your feelings. The sooner you do, the sooner you will be able to get on with the important task of finding a new job and moving ahead with new challenges. Do *not* let money worries stand in the way of getting professional help to deal with your feelings. The longer you wait, the longer you will be likely to be unable to start your job search. Most communities have several organizations that offer professional counseling at reduced rates. Get out your Yellow Pages and look for any one of these:

> *Local mental health centers.* Almost every major city has a local mental health and guidance center that offers coun-

seling services for a reduced fee. Look in your Yellow Pages under "Mental Health Services."

Local churches. Churches of any denomination don't care if you are a member when you are in need of help. Most churches have support groups for unemployed people, especially during difficult economic times. If you need additional counseling, church staff members can refer you to organizations that can offer low-cost counseling services.

YW/YMCA. Most YW/YMCA organizations have a counseling center or can refer you to helpful organizations in your community.

Local psychological associations and hospital referral services. Most psychological associations have a referral number you can use to get access to professional counseling. Look in your Yellow Pages under "Associations." Many major hospitals in large cities now publicize physician referral services you can call to get help.

Above all, remember that suicide is a permanent answer to a very temporary problem. You and your family will survive this situation, and your career may actually benefit in the long run. Find a competent counselor to talk with so that you can get on with the important work of finding a new job.

Get Moving Right Away

Some of the advice friends will give you when you are out of work can be helpful. Other times their advice should definitely be ignored. One of the worst ideas when you have been laid off is to "take some time off. Relax! You've earned it." In fact, the longer you wait to find a job, the longer it will take, and the more likely you will be to dwell on your situation. Your new job will not find you. Every day that you wait before starting is just one more day you go without a job.

Bob Shea, president of an outplacement firm in Virginia, tells people to start looking right away. As difficult as it may seem, he believes the best advice is to act immediately. "You've got to set your emotions aside and get about the business of marketing yourself for the next job," Shea believes. Even though you will definitely experience some strong emotions, you cannot let your emotions stand in the way of finding a new job.

BEING HONEST WITH YOUR FAMILY

If the best way to survive the ordeal of being out of work is to get help from others, the best place to start is within your own family. If you are married and have one or more children, the added responsibility of being at least partly responsible for their financial security can weigh on you. On the other hand, if you are honest with your family and talk with them about what to expect, you can all help each other get through this time together.

Immediately after you lose your job, you have two primary tasks: outlining your budget and organizing your job search. If you have a family, you need to involve them as much as possible in the process. Everything you do, every choice you make, affects them. You need to be honest with your spouse about your current financial situation. You both need to agree how you will weather this storm, what you will do without and how much of your savings you will use how quickly. In addition, as you define your job search, your spouse needs to understand what role he or she can play in helping you find a new job. He or she can help by doing some typing or proofreading, by answering the telephone, or by helping you network.

What Do I Tell the Kids?

If you have children, you and your spouse need to decide how and what to tell them about your current job situation. The important thing to remember is that different children will accept the situation differently, but most children are sensitive to changes in the family. You need to keep the lines of communication open so that your children understand what's happening and how it affects them. You also need to be aware of how your attitudes and emotions can affect them while you are unemployed.

Dr. Marlene Schmidt is a child psychiatrist. "Children at different ages will react differently to one parent's loss of a job," Dr. Schmidt explains. "It will be helpful to understand how children at different ages may react so you can talk with them in a way that they will understand."

Infants through Age 2 or 3 Infants and very young children (through age 2 or 3) likely do not need to be told anything at all. Rather, the most important thing to remember in dealing with young children during a time of family stress is that you as a parent may be more easily frustrated and less patient with young children. "Especially if you have a colicky or fussy baby," Dr. Schmidt warns, "your capacity to soothe the child may be limited by the fact that you are already under a great deal of stress." In addition, if you are not used to spending a great deal of time with an infant or small child, the sudden responsibility can be daunting.

You need to be aware that your fuse may be short at times, and be careful that your child doesn't suffer as a result. If you aren't used to it and feel increasingly frustrated with the stress of caring for a very small child, you need to ask for help from friends or family members. "Plan times for the child to spend time away from you," Dr. Schmidt advises. Friends, family, or neighbors can help by babysitting in their homes for a few hours every other day or so. Not only will this help reduce the stress level on you and your child, it will also give you time to concentrate on your job search efforts.

Preschool-Age Children Preschool-age children (ages 3 through 5) understand more about what is going on within the family and may ask more questions about mom or dad being home when he or she is not supposed to be. "The important thing to remember with children in this age group," Dr. Schmidt explains, "is that they can tend to think in magical terms. If something bad happens to the family, they think they somehow caused it to happen."

You need to demystify the situation for children in this age group. Explain what has happened in simple, concrete terms that they can understand. Be sure you emphasize the fact that the problem happened, that they did *not* cause it in any way, and that mom and dad are responsible for fixing it and will take care of it. A child at this age needs to understand that something has changed, that mom and dad may seem upset from time to time, but that it is not because of something the child did.

Children at this age can also be very sensitive to changes in the status of their primary caregiver. If a 3- or 4-year-old is used to being home with mom every day, but now mom must find a job to help financially, the child can react with anger and withdrawal. "If this happens," Dr. Schmidt advises, "don't blame yourself. Your child can adjust to the situation over time."

Ages 5 through 9 At this age, children are more resilient and adaptable. They learn about rules and games and are better able to understand more complex thoughts, and to articulate their own thoughts and feelings. Although you may want to protect young children from the reality of the situation, you should be aware that children are very perceptive at many levels. They will sense and be aware that something is wrong, even if you don't tell them.

One family with a 7-year-old boy decided not to burden the

child with the news that his father had been fired. Instead, they explained that "daddy will be working at home for a while." As several months passed and his father was still unemployed, the stress level within the family rose. Both parents worried and argued more than usual. Because they never explained to their son exactly what was going on, he created reasons in his mind to explain his parents' arguments. When asked by a school psychologist about what was happening at home, the boy told her he was sure his father was dying of cancer.

This story illustrates the fact that children at this age will know that something is wrong. If you are not honest with them, they will create explanations of their own that can cause them more stress than the real reasons for the family's current problems. In addition, if you are not honest with your children, you may be teaching them not to come to *you* when *they* have problems.

Again, you need to find a simple way to explain the situation to children in this age group. "Children in this age group tend to learn better through metaphors," Dr. Schmidt explains. You can explain to them that mom's or dad's job loss was something like a game of musical chairs or a car that ran out of gas. Put it in simple terms that they can understand, but don't try to hide the situation from them altogether.

Preadolescent and Adolescent Children   Children between the ages of 12 and 18 are better able to understand the problems associated with the loss of a job. In addition, they also look to the future more and will personally feel the financial risks involved. Because clothes and other status symbols can be very important to teenaged children, the loss of income can create a great deal of anxiety for them.

You need to be very clear with teenagers. If your job loss will have a significant impact on their lives, they need to understand the situation and its impact. If your college-bound daughter is not already looking at less expensive local public colleges, you must discuss the future with her as soon as possible. Be as straightforward as possible in explaining the situation to them.

You should also be aware that teenaged children may likely react with anger or resentment when they discover that the family's sudden financial changes will have a direct impact on them. This sudden anger, and the guilt it may elicit in you, can exacerbate an already difficult situation. As with any family crisis, you need to keep the lines of communication open. Be sure you let them talk about how they feel and how the situation affects them.

Family Help

Job loss and the stress it causes can have significant effects on a family. If your children start to experience problems as a result, you may need to seek family counseling. Some warning signs may become apparent, highlighting the need for professional help. You may start to notice personality changes in a younger child: He or she was once playful and cheerful and is now lethargic or angry and inconsolable. Older children and teenagers may have problems at school, show dramatic personality changes, or may start having appetite and sleep problems.

If your family situation becomes severely disrupted and you are worried about the impact on your children, you should seek professional help. Family counselors are trained to help families communicate better, especially during stressful times. If you need help, call any one of the agencies mentioned earlier in this chapter.

MAKING DECISIONS

As this chapter has illustrated, sudden job loss can have a devastating impact on you and your family. As with any traumatic situation, sudden job loss can affect your ability to make decisions. Because you already have enough major issues to address (what kinds of jobs to look for, how to manage your emergency budget), you should avoid making any decisions you don't need to make right now.

For example, don't buy anything major, such as a car or other expensive items. Don't make decisions about having or adopting another child. Just because you suddenly have more time on your hands, don't take this as a sign that it's a good time to get pregnant. If you make such life-altering decisions during times of extreme stress, you may regret it later. Some things cannot be undone later on, and you'll regret having made the choice at a time when you may not have been terribly rational.

HONEST EXPECTATIONS

As you look for a new job, you need to have some honest expectations of how long it will take and what kind of job you are likely to find. If you are more honest with yourself from the outset, you can avoid some anxiety later on. Chapter 8 discusses how to determine the type of job you are suited for and gives some guidelines on how long a job search may take. Because these guidelines are only averages, your search may take longer or you may find a new job sooner than you think.

The important thing is to be as realistic as possible. Think about some second-or third-choice positions you would be willing to take if the search takes longer than you anticipate. Try to find out as much information as possible about your odds for finding the kind of job you are looking for, and be honest with yourself about your prospects. If you live in an area that is already struggling through a severe recession, you may have to be willing to settle for less than your first-choice position.

If you make some realistic decisions when you start your search and agree on what you can accept, you'll avoid painting yourself into a corner several months later.

4 | For the Understanding Spouse

One man remembers what the days were like during the four months his wife was out of work. "There were days I just dreaded going home," he says. "I didn't know what she'd be like when I got there. If the job search went well that day, and it looked like some doors were opening, she'd have a positive outlook. But on those days that all the doors seemed shut, she'd just seem so hopeless. She really started to believe she'd *never* find another job. Then we'd argue about whether she really was marketable. I'd tell her I knew she wouldn't be out very long and she'd give me a million reasons why this could go on *forever*. It was one of the hardest times in our marriage. I couldn't say it to her, but I kept wondering why she didn't take that job offer she'd had the previous fall. We never would have had to go through this if she had just taken that job before she got laid off."

If your spouse is out of work, you know all about the emotional responses discussed in Chapter 3. You understand the crushing depression, the money anxieties, the concerns over what to tell family and friends. The problem is, this is really your *spouse's* time of need. He or she needs you to be supportive, to say that the money will last, to believe he or she will find a job soon. But who supports you? How do *you* deal with a situation that may be equally as unnerving for you? How do you help with the job search? And what do you do if your spouse seems to have given up on finding another job?

Clearly, one spouse's job loss can be one of the most devastating events a married couple can face. You have financial worries and you have no idea how long this will last. As this chapter will show, the key to dealing with the situation is to understand what your spouse is going through and to be committed to facing the situation as partners. If you can avoid placing blame, act positive, and help keep your spouse's job search on track, you will both fare better through the ordeal. The best way to support your spouse is to have a strong support structure of your own and to keep the lines of communication open. You don't have to be strong all the time; you simply have to find ways of defusing the stress while still maintaining a positive outlook that encourages your spouse's efforts.

HE (SHE) ISN'T HANDLING THIS THE WAY I WOULD

If your spouse is out of work, it might help to try to understand how he or she may be approaching the situation. Men and women can react to job loss very differently, depending on how they were raised and how each sees his or her role in the relationship. As you try to empathize with your spouse's situation, you may need to understand what he or she may be feeling.

What Makes a Man a Man

Most men were raised in a household in which the man made the money and the woman stayed home with the children. Despite years of change in how men and women see their roles, many men still believe they must be the primary provider for their families. If your husband is out of work, he is probably struggling with the fact that he is not fulfilling his responsibilities. "It's my job, not *hers*," he may be thinking. "I'm the one who is responsible for this family."

A psychologist specializing in family therapy, Dr. Eileen Raffaniello, believes, "Men's self-image can be wrapped up in what they do to the extent that they are ashamed and even embarrassed to let anyone know they are out of work. Their ideas of what 'makes a man a man' can make it difficult for them to accept help in dealing with the situation, especially if they have defined a more traditional relationship in their own marriages."

Your husband may find it difficult to even admit to other men that he is out of work, much less talk with them about how the situation makes him feel. He'll likely try to avoid talking with friends and family altogether. One man remembered that the one person he couldn't tell about his job loss was his father. "It took me three weeks to screw up the courage to tell him I was out of work. My dad worked for the same company for 36 years. He was the perfect breadwinner. How could I tell him that my wife was now supporting my family?"

Withdrawing from family and friends may be the easiest way for your husband to deal with the situation. However, that can place an unrealistic burden on you. If your husband reacts by withdrawing, you will need to help him stay in contact with male friends and relatives and not avoid them. He needs to understand that these people can not only provide a strong sense of support, they are also a key part of his job-search network. Rather than react with shame or scorn, he'll most likely find that his family and friends understand the situation much more than he thinks. "I couldn't believe it," one man recalls, "when I finally told two of my Kiwanis buddies I was out of work, their reaction was, 'Yeah, so who *hasn't* been?' *Everyone* knows someone who's been out of work."

What Are You Worried About?—You Don't *Need* the Money

Women, on the other hand, bear a different burden when they lose a job. Many career women can find the situation disorienting, especially if they have sacrificed family plans for their career goals. According to Dr. Raffaniello, "They weren't playing the feminine role, and now they feel they've failed at the masculine role as well." The difficulty for many women who put their careers first and find themselves suddenly out of work is that they have trouble justifying their past choices, not only to themselves but also to family members.

In addition, people may actually be less sympathetic towards a woman who is unemployed. "If I had a nickel for everyone who said to me, 'But you don't really *need* the money,' I wouldn't have *needed* another job," one woman remembers. Friends or relatives may think they know what you and your wife's financial situation is and whether or not the two of you can survive without her income. Regardless of the financial situation, when friends and family dismiss a woman's career simply because she doesn't "need the money," she may feel even more discouraged.

Your wife may find that she is constantly having to explain herself and her choices. If her mother has been waiting years to be a grandmother, your wife may be in for some "I told you so" reactions. Regardless of what changes society has gone through, many people still see women's careers as frivolous extras that can get in the way of women's *real* role: bearing and raising children.

Even though you may be trying to cheer her up, you need to avoid minimizing the loss of your wife's job. If you say, "Hey, honey, we really don't *need* the money," to reduce her money worries, you may also be minimizing the important choices she has made in her life. She needs to hear that her career choices are important and that you believe this is just a temporary setback in her career.

Above all, your wife's job loss should not be seen as a sign that the two of you should start a family or have another child. Unless your wife was planning to leave her job soon to raise children, be careful about using her job loss as an excuse. Job loss is an extremely traumatic situation. You should avoid making major decisions while your wife is out of work.

Common Ground: Forming a Partnership

Having empathy for your husband's or wife's position can go a long way in easing the situation for both of you. Beyond understanding each other's position, though, you need to realize that job loss has happened to *both* of you and that the best way to survive it is to work as partners, partners that support each other, talk to each other, and bear equal shares of the burden for maintaining family security. The rest of this chapter talks about ways to define a partnership to work with your spouse through this difficult time.

As the spouse of someone out of work, your role in the partnership involves a number of key elements. You need to be realistic and positive. You need to take an active, supportive, *non-blaming* role in your spouse's job search. Probably most important of all, you need to pay attention to your own worries so that you can provide the support system your spouse needs.

HOW CAN I BE SUPPORTIVE
WHEN I'M WORRIED MYSELF?

"In the 'for better or worse' category, it was *definitely* one of the 'worse' times," one woman says as she recalls the time her husband was out of work. Unemployment can isolate the person who is out of a job. If your wife spends her days at home sending resumés and making telephone calls, you may be the first person she sees all day. No matter what *your* day was like, when you walk through the door you find that she needs reassurance. You may have spent the day in meetings, thinking about how long you can make the mortgage payments on your salary alone. When you come home, though, you're expected to put all that aside and deal with her worries and concerns.

For some men, their wives are the only people they feel comfortable talking with about feelings and worries. Because men were raised to be breadwinners, being unemployed is an embarrassing situation they may not want to discuss with anyone but their wives. If you are the wife of someone who is unemployed, this can place an unrealistic burden on you to be the sole support of your husband during this time.

Worse yet, your spouse may refuse to accept *anyone's* help, even yours. If you don't know what he's feeling, if she won't discuss her concerns with you at all, you can begin to feel helpless and unable to control the situation.

Developing Your Own Support Network

The key to dealing with this added stress is to be sure you have your own support network. Because you are being called on to be the supportive one at home, you will need to find ways to blow off steam. "One of the most important things my wife's layoff taught me," one man said, "was the need to have outside support and friendships." You'll be amazed at how supportive friends and family can be when you need their help. Spending a few minutes talking with someone you trust before you go home at the end of the day can help you be calmer and more supportive when you get there.

In addition to friends and family, you may find it helpful to talk with professionals who can help you deal with the stress. Your employer may have an employee assistance program that offers free counseling services. Sometimes an objective professional can offer you a place to vent your own anger and frustration before you go home.

In the same way, if you are a member of a church or community organization, find someone there to talk with. You'll be amazed at how many times ministers or people in your community have dealt with similar family problems. Your church may sponsor a support group for unemployed individuals and their families. Find such a group and attend one or two meetings, with or without your spouse. The anxiety, frustration, and anger you are feeling right now are almost universal responses to the kind of stress you are experiencing. One of the easiest ways to defuse the emotional impact on you is to commiserate with others dealing with the same problems.

Find ways to simply blow off steam. Play a rousing game of racquetball with a colleague, plug in an aerobics tape, scream in your car on the way home. Your spouse is not the only one who is angry and frustrated. You need to find ways to relieve your own tension.

Probably most important, no matter how difficult the situation may be at home, don't avoid your spouse. No matter how difficult it is to go home at the end of the day, you do need to be there. Developing a support network outside the home does not mean spending every evening after work out with friends, avoiding the situation at home. Remember, you are partners in solving this problem. The more you work on this problem together, the stronger your relationship can be now and when it's over.

REGRETS AND ANGER

Everyone has regrets about career choices. Your husband turned down a job offer just before he was laid off. Your wife wanted to work for a small company because they "seemed to be more people-oriented." As the days wear on and you ride the job-search roller coaster together, you can't help remembering all the things you or your spouse *should* have done to avoid being in this situation. Worse yet, you may have pushed him or her to leave the company before the situation got worse and your spouse chose to stay.

How do you deal with the regrets you have now? As the anxiety and bills mount, "I told you so" may be a recurring thought. At this point, it's important for you and your spouse to focus on what you *can* do and not on what you should have done. In your own mind, realize that all the past career choices your spouse made are over and that you need to move forward. The worst thing you can do right now is talk about what your spouse *should* have done to avoid this situation.

"The important part about dealing with any stressful situation is to avoid blame," Dr. Raffaniello points out. "Even saying 'It's not your fault' still perpetuates a blaming attitude." Instead, you need to focus on what you both can do to move his or her career forward.

As bleak as your situation may seem now, when it's over you'll soon forget the 'should haves' that helped put you both where you are now. Start now to put them out of your mind. You can't change the future by dwelling on the past and you certainly can't help your spouse by reminding him or her of past decisions that, in light of your current situation, seem like huge mistakes.

Your Husband's Former Employer

Jenny's husband was a manufacturer's representative for more than a dozen years. When his employer refused to deal with a festering personnel problem, Mark and his employer parted company. "Two weeks after my husband and his employer dissolved their business relationship, I realized I was dealing with the situation on a very personal level," Jenny explains. "I felt disbelief and took it very personally. Our families had become close friends over the years and now this happened. I couldn't help feeling angry and hurt by the company's actions."

Especially if your spouse was with his or her former employer for many years, you may feel a great deal of anger toward the company and his or her former managers. You may have a number of friends who still work for the company and who feel they must maintain a loyalty to their employer. Many of these friendships are not only important to you personally, they are also a key part of your spouse's network of contacts as he or she looks for a new position.

The important thing to remember right now is that you need to salvage whatever relationships you can. Because it may be difficult to socialize with people who still work for your spouse's former employer, you may want to avoid social gatherings that involve them right now. Instead, look to other friends for help and advice and avoid situations that can only add to your frustration.

"My husband and I finally decided to avoid parties and gatherings with some of his former colleagues for a while," one woman said. "We learned that it was too difficult for us to spend time with them all the while wondering if they were thinking, 'Why him and not me?' " Though her husband was still able to call on these important business contacts for assistance during his job search, he and his wife felt more comfortable keeping these relationships at a distance.

There may be some relationships that are too damaged to ever salvage. "After Mark was no longer working for the company," Jenny recalls, "the president's wife sent me a letter saying she hoped this wouldn't hurt our friendship and that she'd still like to have us out to the house 'sometime soon.' I haven't answered that letter yet. I had to wait until I could be rational enough to tell her what I want to say. Right now I'm just too angry."

Regardless of the reasons behind your spouse's departure, you may never be able to quite forgive his or her former employer. Be aware that you may lose a few friendships in the process but that you should work hard to at least maintain a professional relationship with people who can help with your spouse's career plans.

BE HONEST ABOUT THE MONEY

"All I could think when my husband told me about the layoff," Joan remembers, "was that we were going to lose the house. I had never dealt with any of the financial details. All I knew was that the bank had approved the loan on the basis of *both* our incomes. I had no idea how we could make it." In her mind, this woman had created a scenario that was actually much worse than reality.

In most marriages, one person handles most of the financial details. This works well as long as things go according to plan. When one of you is out of work, your financial picture changes drastically. Many couples who have experienced unemployment quickly learn that information about finances can be crucial to both the person who has lost a job and to his or her spouse.

If you are out of work and your husband always handles the finances, make sure you look at the budget together. Your wife may have always paid the bills because you hate dealing with financial details. Your current situation makes it important for *both* of you to clearly understand your financial picture.

Chapter 6 describes a simple process for developing a family budget to deal with this emergency. The most important part of the process for married couples is to do it *together*. During times of extreme financial stress, information can be your most important asset. If you both understand your financial picture and both agree on what you can and cannot do without, you can help avoid arguments down the road. You may have to readjust the plan as you go along, but the important thing is to make these decisions together to avoid unnecessary friction.

"Once he showed me the whole picture," Joan recalls, "I was relieved. I even felt a little foolish that until that time I had absolutely *no* idea how much we actually had in savings. Just knowing the true picture helped me sleep better."

LISTEN

"I've learned to be a much better listener," Jenny believes. Like other people whose spouses have struggled with job loss, she has found that sometimes it's important just to listen rather than offer advice or try to solve her husband's problems. Being out of work may give you both a chance to talk about things you never have a chance to discuss. Your spouse may have hated his or her line of work for a long time and never talked about it with you. Or he or she may have had dreams you never knew about, such as starting a business.

If your spouse has lost a job, he or she is struggling with a grief process. Sometimes it can help for you to listen to the emotions and simply accept them. The irony of tragedy in a marriage is that it can give you a chance to open new lines of communication.

Because he was a manufacturer's representative, Jenny's husband had traveled extensively. Now that he was home more often, they actually had more time to talk with each other. "Even though I worry all the time," she confesses, "I've found a peacefulness in being able to be this close to Mark."

FOCUS ON THE POSITIVE

The lows can get pretty low. There are days you may feel you don't even *recognize* this person you live with. What happened to the executive who could handle everything? What happened to the up-and-coming corporate star who had the world by the tail? Because job loss has a devastating effect on self-esteem, the impact on your spouse will be great. There will be days when he'll just wallow in his own hopelessness, when she'll pick a fight with you the minute you walk through the door.

As you face your spouse's raw emotional responses, you'll need to keep building a positive emotional framework for him or her. You need to affirm the reality of the situation, helping your spouse realize that his or her feelings are not fact. Unemployed people tend to shift between extremes, either catastrophizing or minimizing their situation. Strong, positive statements reaffirming your spouse's fine qualities help build a more realistic picture.

"You were good enough to get the last job. You're good enough to get the next one," one wife repeatedly told her husband while he was out of work. He couldn't argue with the reality: He *had* been good enough to get the last job.

Once you develop a budget, you can use it as a strong tool in your campaign to accentuate the positive. Remind your spouse that you worked out the financial concerns and that you will be able to take care of each other. Time *is* on your side, this will *not* go on forever, and you have both agreed on a financial plan that will tide you through. Remind your spouse that he or she *does* have a job right now—finding another job. The more he or she can focus on his or her positive qualities, the quicker that will happen.

As you focus on the positive, you can also talk about the positive aspects of the fact that your spouse no longer works for his or her former employer. Especially if your spouse's former employer had financial problems for a long period of time, he or she may actually be relieved not to be under that stress. You can help him or her focus on the future, on potential employers that are more financially stable, on companies that offer him or her more room for professional growth.

"Mark just *looked* better," Jenny pointed out. "Almost immediately after he severed the relationship with his company, he looked better and he felt better. The stress of an unreasonable situation was finally lifted off his shoulders."

Remind your spouse that the two of you have been through difficult times before and that you will work through this together. "I kept telling her that the job wasn't as important as the fact that we would get through this," one man said, remembering his wife's low times. "I'd say it at least once a day: 'If we can get through this, we can get through anything.'"

KEEP A SENSE OF HUMOR

Make it your goal to make your spouse laugh at least once a day. Rent a movie you know will force at least a smile. Get a picture of his or her former boss (or the company's logo) and put it on a dart board in the family room. Take turns to see who has the better shot. Make a "Top 10 List" of your favorite management blunders perpetrated by your spouse's former employer. Record the dumbest responses you've heard from friends or family when you told them one of you lost a job. Spend time talking about the worst date you ever had.

The point is, laughter can help relieve tension, and it will help you both forget your situation for a moment. Laughter may be your best—some days your *only*—weapon in a situation that can seem completely out of control.

FEELING NEEDED

Because your spouse may seem fragile during this time, you may react by trying to protect him or her. You need to be careful not to overprotect. "Don't treat him or her like an invalid or incompetent simply because he or she is out of a job," Dr. Raffaniello warns. Your spouse needs to feel needed, perhaps more than usual. This doesn't mean you should come up with a list of menial tasks for him or her to complete "because you're home anyway." Rather, don't be afraid to look to your spouse for the kind of advice you normally seek.

Don't be afraid that, by asking for counsel and opinions, you are placing too much of a burden on him or her. More than likely, your spouse will welcome the chance to feel needed. "It's okay to come home at the end of the day and say 'I really had a lousy day. Can I talk to you about it?'" Dr. Raffaniello believes. Rather than see it as a burden, your spouse may see it as a chance to help solve a problem and forget about job-search worries for a while.

HE (SHE) WON'T LET ME HELP

"It's *my* problem to solve, not hers," one man told a family counselor. "A man is supposed to take care of his wife, not be a burden." A woman who lost her job bristled when her teacher husband suggested he could postpone the summer class he planned to take and get a summer job instead.

Because your spouse is already feeling a loss of self-worth, he or she may be indignant about you assuming even more of the financial burden than you've already assumed. It may make you feel better to say, "He can't work, so I will," but it may make your spouse feel even worse.

The fact may be, though, that you *do* need the money. You may feel angry and frustrated that your spouse's stubborn pride is getting in the way of providing for your family. You need to find a way to help any way you can while still allowing your spouse to rebuild his or her damaged self-esteem.

Once again, the solution to the problem is to remind your spouse that you are in this situation as *partners*. From the beginning of his or her unemployment, you have to agree that you will both do whatever it takes to protect your family and help your spouse find a new job quickly. Rather than saying, "Hey, *somebody* has to be earning some money," you need to remind your spouse of your agreement to work together. "This problem belongs to *both* of us and we need to work *together* to solve it. I hope that, if it ever happens to me, you'll be creative about finding other sources of income and I'll be smart enough to let you."

WHEN YOUR SPOUSE ISN'T LOOKING HARD ENOUGH

"Greg really had a hard time getting started with his job search after he was fired," Martha remembers. "It was as if he didn't know where to begin. I'd come home at the end of the day and he would have spent the whole day straightening out the drawers in his office or transplanting houseplants. He never seemed to *accomplish* anything. I wasn't sure how to pressure him to do anything. I was afraid if I said anything he'd get angry and defensive. In the meantime, all I did was worry. If he didn't get started soon, he'd never have a job before his severance pay ran out."

The days are slipping by, your spouse's severance pay is running out, and he or she is still trying to decide on the perfect resumé style. One of two factors may be operating here: Either your spouse is too devastated by his or her situation to be able to get started, or he or she may just be a procrastinator at heart. For some people, both factors may contribute to an inability to get started or to keep looking when the signs seem discouraging. Between the two of you, you need to come to terms on how the job search will proceed. You need to start with some realistic ideas of both your expectations.

Negotiating Job-Search Terms

Once again, you and your spouse need to form a partner-ship when it comes to solving the problem of his or her un-employment. This is especially true when it comes to defining the methods he or she will use to look for a job. The two of you together need to read Chapter 7, put together a plan for the whole process of looking for a job, and stay on track with the plan.

Be as specific as you possibly can: Decide how many days your spouse should spend assessing his or her past positions and deciding what kind of positions to look for. After deciding on positions and what companies to target, set aside a Saturday morning to brainstorm on the names to include in a job-search network. Decide how much time it will take him or her to develop an effective resumé. Agree on dates by which he or she will have contacted each person in his or her network.

Decide what parts of the plan will be *your* responsibility. After all, you are in this together. You can help by taking over some of the menial tasks for your husband or wife: typing re-sumés, stuffing envelopes, organizing a tickler file for the network of contacts. Be sure you are both actively involved in the job-search process.

In short, create a project plan for the job search and work together to make sure that it happens. If you are working during the day, agree on one or two times each day when you will call each other to talk about that day's accomplishments. Agree to set aside at least one half-hour every night for a status meeting. Talk about what works well and what needs to be improved.

Not only will an active plan help your spouse find a job more quickly, you will also both feel in control of the situation. In some ways, finding another job is simply a numbers game. If you and your spouse are busy making contacts and sending resumés, neither of you will have as much time to worry about your present situation.

Work Together to Eliminate Distractions

Right now, finding another job *is* your spouse's job. You and the rest of the family need to be sure nothing gets in the way of that task. You may have decided that you can save money on day care by leaving the kids home with dad during the day. The money you save may be negated by the fact that he spends more time with them than he does looking for another job. If the children are old enough to understand, they must be told that, for a set number of hours each day, no one is to bother your spouse. They need to understand that mom or dad is "at work" during those hours and should only be bothered during an absolute emergency.

If your children are not old enough to understand these kinds of limits, you may have to come up with an alternative form of child care temporarily. You may have to ask for help from neighbors or friends one or two days each week or you may have to hire a baby-sitter for a few hours each day. Whatever money you spend will be an investment in reducing the amount of time your spouse is out of work.

Finally, don't load your spouse's schedule with a list of chores you haven't had time to get to lately. His or her job is to find a new job, not to spend time fixing that stuck window or replacing the screen on the kitchen door. If there are a few tasks he or she would like to accomplish while out of work, agree that they will only be tackled after each day's job-search plans are completed.

Just Take a Job, *Any* Job

"I didn't care what kind of job she found after a while. I just wanted it to be over," one man lamented of his wife's job search. Because you aren't the one looking for a job, it is easier for you to discount some of your spouse's job-search criteria. As you both agree on job-search criteria, you may need to also agree on what types of positions would be acceptable second choices, and how soon you would both start to consider one of those second-choice positions.

Again, if you agree in advance how long you can last financially, you can set some reasonable limits for accepting a second- or third-choice position if the job search takes longer than you anticipated. You and your spouse both need to remember that your chief goal should be finding a position that is a good fit for him or her and that also provides your family with the financial security you've agreed you need. If he or she cannot find a first-choice position in a reasonable time frame, however, your spouse may need to agree to accept something less than his or her ideal job.

As with every part of the unemployment problem, you need to discuss all options together and come to reasonable conclusions about what you both find acceptable. The earlier you start to make these agreements with each other, the easier it will be for both of you to deal with the uncertainties of your spouse's job search.

GETTING HELP

Even if you are supporting your spouse and you both have a strong support network, you may need outside help in dealing with the impact of job loss on each of you individually and on your marriage. Depression and a loss of self-esteem are almost universal reactions to the loss of a job. If you or your spouse become debilitated by the emotions, or if you fear your marriage may not be able to withstand the stress, you should look for professional help.

Warning Signs

The most important warning sign to look for is any sign of suicidal thoughts. Studies have shown that the risk of suicide can increase dramatically for someone who is unemployed. If your spouse starts saying he or she would be "better off dead" or that you would be better off with the insurance money, get professional help *at once*.

Although your husband or wife may not be suicidal, the devastation of losing a job may make it difficult for him or her to cope and move ahead with job-search plans. If his or her depression becomes debilitating, you will need to seek professional help. Look for classic signs of severe depression: Your spouse may be unable to cope with even small tasks, and he or she may completely lose hope. At the same time, a depressed person can completely resist anyone's attempts to help him or her. If your husband's or wife's depression becomes severe, you need to seek professional help.

In addition to your spouse's reactions, you need to be aware of how the situation affects you and your marriage. If your own anxiety or depression becomes so severe that you are unable to cope, you need to find professional help for yourself. In the same way, if your marriage is in danger, if you argue constantly with no resolution, or if your begin to avoid your spouse altogether, you need to seek the advice of a professional counselor.

Where to Go for Help

Most importantly, don't think that professional counseling is one of the things you can just do without during a time of financial strain. There are a number of agencies and community organizations that offer completely confidential counseling services for a reduced fee. Some of the available options are:

Local mental health centers. Almost every major city has a local mental health and guidance center that offers counseling services for a reduced fee. Look in your Yellow Pages under "Mental Health Services."

Local churches. Churches of any denomination don't care if you are a member when you are in need of help. Most churches have support groups for unemployed people, especially during difficult economic times. If you need additional counseling, church staff members can refer you to organizations that can offer low-cost counseling services.

YW/YMCA. Most YW/YMCA organizations have a counseling center or can refer you to helpful organizations in your community.

Local psychological associations and hospital referral services. Most psychological associations have a referral number you can use to get access to professional counseling. Look in your Yellow Pages under "Associations." Many major hospitals in large cities now publicize physician referral services you can call to get help.

The Better Business Bureau. If you and your spouse have always had trouble handling finances, the consumer division of the Better Business Bureau can put you in touch with counselors who can provide low-cost money management advice and assistance. If your credit cards were already up to the limit when your spouse was laid off, run, don't walk, to a credit counselor's office.

5 | The Unemployment Office

One previously unemployed woman remembers her experience with the unemployment office: "I never thought I'd ever find myself in the unemployment office. I was there on December 18, one week before Christmas. If I was a director and wanted to film a scene in a government office, I would have picked this place. When I walked in the door, someone told me to take a number. It was 2:30 in the afternoon and they were on number 164. I looked down at the slip of paper in my hand and read the number. 297. I laughed out loud and 133 pairs of eyes turned to look at me. I waited until nearly 5:00 before they called my number. The fourth time I was on the phone to my husband they called my number. The people behind me whose numbers were not called by 5:00 were told to come back the next day."

Unemployment compensation is a benefit the government provides unemployed people. Getting that compensation when you need it can be a trial in itself. You not only have to overcome your own pride ("I won't take charity!"), you also have to deal with a variety of rules and regulations that seem to be designed to keep you from receiving the compensation you need.

Unemployment compensation rules are definitely a maze—with money at the end. Although this chapter isn't a guide to unemployment compensation laws in any particular state, it will help you know what to be prepared for as you apply for benefits that are, by all rights, something you have earned as a working member of society. In general, unemployment compensation rules are very similar from one state to the next. Forty-one states follow the Wage Record System, designed to make application procedures the same from one state to the next and to facilitate cross-state claims.

Unemployment forms are not as complicated as health insurance forms and certainly much less complex than IRS tax forms. With a little planning and some investigation, you can work your way through the maze and get the compensation you and your family need.

THE TEN MOST IMPORTANT THINGS

The rest of this chapter is organized as a "Top Ten List" of things to do and not to do when you apply for unemployment compensation. You'll likely need support during the process and this chapter describes the support you can look for and expect as you file your claim. Many people have been through the process of applying for unemployment compensation. Some of them say the best thing to do is try to retain a sense of humor and remember that you're dealing with a huge government bureaucracy. Based on past experience, then, all you need to know is listed below:

The Ten Most Important Things to Remember When Applying for Unemployment Insurance

1. Swallow Your Pride

2. Apply Right Away

3. Take a Friend

4. Know How Much You Should Be Getting

5. Understand the Rules

6. Be Patient—This Will Take Some Time

7. Always Do Everything Exactly as They Say

8. The Bureau of Employment Services Should Really Be Called "Forms-R-Us"

9. Appeal a Bad Decision

10. Know the Tax Laws

Swallow Your Pride

For some people, the most difficult part of applying for unemployment compensation is convincing themselves to do it. "I don't take charity from anyone!" How many times have you made this statement or heard it from your parents? Most of our parents grew up during or immediately after the Great Depression, an era of economic uncertainty that created immense anxiety many people have carried with them throughout their lives. Memories of that time stuck with those who survived the Great Depression.

In times such as those, often all people had left was their pride. Before unemployment insurance or other state assistance existed, people's only recourse was to survive on their own or to "take charity" from family members, their local church, or other community organizations. Accepting such charity was unthinkable to many people then. Unfortunately that attitude has been passed to the next generation, making it difficult for some people to apply for government benefits when they need them.

There are two very important reasons to apply for unemployment compensation: first, you need it; second, the company that laid you off pays for it.

If you've just lost a job, your own feelings of self-worth may be taking it on the chin. Applying for unemployment compensation may make you feel as though you have failed in some way. As you struggle with these feelings and concerns, remember that you are doing something that is best for your family. You do need the money. Even though you've lost a job, the rest of the world continues: Bills arrive, schools charge for books, dentists find cavities. If you think of unemployment compensation as an essential part of your family's well-being, you will realize that their survival is more important than your concerns over accepting what may seem like a handout.

"Every time I had to go to the unemployment office I'd dress to the nines," one woman recalls. "I was making a statement. I wanted people to think that this was just a temporary thing, that I really didn't belong in the unemployment line. Most of all, I wanted to believe it myself."

The second important reason to apply for unemployment compensation is that *the company that laid you off pays for it*. Unemployment compensation was legislated as a result of massive unemployment in the 1930s. The federal government designed the overall compensation system, allowing individual states to make changes to the basic formula. The basic formula, though, operates like any other kind of insurance a business purchases to insure itself against harm. The only difference is that businesses are required by law to participate in the insurance program.

Under laws that govern unemployment compensation, a company must pay into the insurance system proportional to the need that the company creates. In other words, a company that consistently fires a lot of people will have to pay higher unemployment compensation premiums. However, the only way the unemployment office knows that an individual has been laid off is if that person applies for compensation. In other words, if you *don't* apply for compensation, you are actually doing your former employer a favor by allowing him or her to pay lower insurance premiums than the law actually allows. Think of it this way: When you apply for compensation, the company's premiums go up. Not that a revenge motive should operate here, but it can be a great way to vent some of your anger!

In short, by working for the company that let you go, you have earned the benefit of unemployment compensation. Philosophically, there is absolutely no difference between unemployment compensation and the medical or dental benefits you received as an employee. The only difference is that you can only use the unemployment benefit when you are out of work. In fact, most employees never use this important company "benefit."

The same is true of unemployment compensation. Your company paid into the system. When you are unemployed and need the money, you get your chance to get something back. You need the money and you've earned it. The only thing left to do is apply for it.

Apply Right Away

As difficult as it may be to think about going to the unemployment office, you should definitely apply immediately after you receive notice that your job is being terminated. In most states, you will not begin to receive unemployment checks until you have been out of work for a number of weeks *after you apply* for compensation. In some states, the period you must wait before receiving checks is only one week. Others require no wait at all. Still others require a wait of as much as two weeks after you apply before you begin receiving unemployment checks.

In addition, your claim may be contested for any one of a number of reasons. (See "Understand the Rules" later in this chapter.) The longer you wait before filing your initial claim, the longer you will have to wait to receive compensation should your claim be delayed for any reason.

Also, to get through the process as quickly as possible, you may want to find out which unemployment offices in your area process the most claims. You may be able to file a claim at any office, regardless of the county you live in. If so, you can avoid offices in the center of a major metropolitan area. An office that's a little off the beaten path in another county may cost you a 30-minute drive while it also saves you a three-hour wait.

Along the same lines, don't delay applying because you're "sure you'll find another job right away." For whatever reason, your expectations may be incorrect and you may lose hundreds of dollars because you waited before applying. You'll feel a little strange about the idea of going to the unemployment office, but you need to do it as soon as possible to receive benefits quickly.

Take a Friend

"I remember the look on Martha's face when I walked into the unemployment office and saw her standing there," one recently unemployed writer remembered. "She was laid off the same day I was. I was wearing a large hat and she had on a pair of sunglasses—indoors. We both laughed when we realized each other's vain attempt at a disguise."

If you've been laid off with a group, make an outing of the unemployment office. Nothing helps ease the situation like black humor shared among friends who have all suffered the same fate. Two heads are also better than one, especially when you're dealing with a bureaucracy. If you're the spouse of someone who's just lost a job, call in sick and go with him or her. Your show of support will go a long way to ease an experience he or she may be dreading.

Know How Much You Should Be Getting

Before you apply for compensation, you can calculate approximately how much to expect. Most states pay unemployment compensation in weekly amounts; these weekly amounts are calculated using a formula that takes into account your average base pay and several factors governing minimum and maximum payments.

In general, you can expect to receive 50 percent of your weekly base pay, up to a certain maximum. Some states pay a higher percentage of your base pay, up to two-thirds, but most pay approximately 50 percent. Many states place a maximum limit on the weekly amount you can receive which, in most states, is less than $200 per week for someone with no dependents. The amount you receive may also depend on other factors, such as the number of people in your family. However, in general, if you had no dependents and were earning more than $400 per week before you were laid off, you can expect to receive less than $200 in unemployment compensation.

One other important note: In most states you can continue to receive a portion of your benefits even if you find a part-time job. As long as the part-time position pays you less than your total benefit amount, most states will pay you the difference between your part-time pay and your benefit amount. Because of this rule, you may be able to get your foot in the door, part time, with a new employer. If the part-time position leads to something more permanent, you've found a new position and earned some money without sacrificing the benefits available to you.

In addition to maximum benefit limits, most states limit the number of weeks in any one benefit year that you can receive benefits. You will be limited to a maximum total benefit amount in any one benefit year. Most states limit the number of weeks in a benefit year to 26 (approximately six months).

Understand the Rules

There are dozens of misconceptions about unemployment compensation. The process can be confusing for most people. "The problem," according to Donald Sheehan, manager of an Ohio Bureau of Employment Services office, "is that we're speaking

Bureaucratise and you're speaking American." According to Shee-han, it helps to ask as many questions as it takes to get the information you need. "Sometimes people feel foolish asking a question," he believes. Rather than ask a question, they'll make a mistake on a form and delay their claim. In general, a number of simple rules of thumb will help you as you apply for compensation.

Do most states make a distinction between being fired and being laid off? It depends. If you were laid off because your company is experiencing financial problems, you are eligible for benefits. If you are fired, your eligibility depends on the reasons behind the firing. In general, your employer has to be able to prove that you are guilty of some kind of misconduct to make you ineligible for benefits.

Personality conflicts and disagreements with your boss do not necessarily count as misconduct. You basically have to be caught stealing from the company, sabotaging your employer, or assaulting one of your co-workers to be fired for misconduct. You should also know that for an action to be considered misconduct it has to be related to your work. If you are caught driving under the influence and your company finds out and fires you, you cannot be considered to have been fired for misconduct (unless, of course, you were driving a delivery van at the time). It's also important to note that even if you are fired for some sort of misconduct, many states still provide benefits, although some may charge you a penalty for misconduct.

What if I left on my own? In some instances, you may lose your job voluntarily because an employer does something that makes it difficult, if not impossible, for you to stay. In that case, you cannot claim you were laid off by the company. However, if your former employer created conditions in which it was difficult for you to continue working, most states will treat your departure in the same way they treat a layoff.

Reasons vary from state to state, but if you were being sexually harassed, asked to work in unsafe conditions, or asked to perform tasks that were well outside of the job you were hired to do, most states consider your departure justifiable.

What other conditions will the state place on my eligibility? The unemployment compensation system has some built-in incentives designed to motivate people to look for a new job. As part of this incentive program, while you receive unemployment compensation you have to be capable of working, available for work, and actively seeking employment. Many states will require you to keep a log of companies to which you've sent a resumé or application.

Can the state force me to accept a job that doesn't suit me? The answer to this question depends on your definition of the word suitable. More to the point, it depends on the state's definition of the word suitable. Most states apply reasonable criteria to determine how suitable a job offer is for you. If you were a manager of an accounting group earning $45,000 per year, the state won't expect you to accept the first $20,000 bookkeeping job offered to you. In most cases, a job offered to you must provide similar wages, work hours, and working conditions to be considered suitable. If you refuse to accept a suitable offer, you can lose your unemployment benefits.

Can I receive unemployment compensation while receiving other sources of income? Once again, it depends on the other source of income. If you take paid vacation time as your severance package, you will likely not be able to receive benefits until after your severance period. If you continue to receive income instead of notification of termination, you will not be able to apply for benefits even if you know that after a certain period of time your position will be terminated. Even if you receive severance pay as a lump-sum payment, the unemployment office may spread that over a number of weeks (based on your most recent weekly salary), making you ineligible for benefits until after that period.

Sources of income *other than* wages will not affect your eligibility. You can receive unemployment compensation while still receiving income from real estate, interest, dividends, and any of a number of nonwage sources.

Will the number of dependents I have affect the amount I receive? Yes, to a point. Many states limit the number of dependents you can claim when filing. If you have dependents, however, you will generally receive a higher weekly amount than someone who has none. If your spouse works, you may or may not be able to claim him or her as a dependent. Most states use a formula, based on both your incomes, to determine if your spouse can be counted as a dependent.

If I owe money, can creditors attach my unemployment compensation? Luckily, the answer to this question is, for all practical purposes, no. When you're unemployed, you're more likely to be concerned about debts you've incurred. Although a creditor can get a judgement to go after any other sources of income you may have, they cannot attach your unemployment compensation. You should be careful to use your unemployment checks for necessities, however. If you deposit your check into a central checking or savings account, and a creditor attaches your accounts, the creditor may be able to take your unemployment compensation as part of the attachment on those accounts. For more information on dealing with creditors, see Chapter 6.

Be Patient—This Will Take Some Time

When you go to the unemployment office for the first time, realize that the trip will probably take several hours. Because the unemployment office is a government office with limited resources, you may have to wait quite a while to simply submit your claim. Several other processes (such as an individual interview, video-tape presentations, or training) make take place on the day you file, or you may be required to return at a later date for these follow-up tasks.

Some people believe the best time to apply is first thing in the morning. This strategy works only if you are willing to arrive early, up to a half-hour before the office opens. Cold winter mornings usually play havoc with this strategy. Late in the day can be a good time to apply as well, because many people believe you have to get there early to get in line right away. If you try this approach, don't arrive any later than 2:00 P.M. because if your number isn't called, you will be sent home and told to come back the next day. Government employees generally don't work overtime.

As for particular days of the week, Donald Sheehan explains that his office receives a larger number of new claims on Monday. Later in the week the numbers tend to decrease. "Friday is definitely the best day," he believes.

Whichever time you choose, take something with you to pass the time you'll spend waiting. Read a book, crochet an afghan, or work on your resumé. You'll feel less frustrated with the wait if you accomplish something in the process.

Always Do Everything Exactly as They Say

This conversation actually took place in an unemployment office:

> Woman behind the desk: "Let's see. You wrote here that you were a marketing manager, right?"
>
> Woman applying: "Yes. That's right."
>
> Woman behind the desk: "Hmmm. Here it says you refuse to work second or third shift. Why is that?"

Woman applying: "Well, I didn't think it made sense. There is no such thing as a 'second shift' job in marketing management."

Woman behind the desk: "Well, you're limiting yourself."

Woman applying: "But there's no such thing as 'shift work' for what I do."

Woman behind the desk: "Ma'am, if you won't cooperate with the process, it may affect your eligibility."

Woman applying: "OK. I give up. You tell me how to play the game and I'll do it."

Woman behind the desk: "This is *not* a game. What you put in these spaces will affect your eligibility."

Woman applying: "OK. Please tell me what I should do."

Woman behind the desk: "Change your answer to 'yes' on this question. Then initial it."

You will undoubtedly encounter such contradictions when you apply for unemployment compensation. It's not a game, but it *is* a game. As in any bureaucratic process, the forms, conventions, and rules that have been developed over the years have taken on a life of their own. You have to realize in advance that these Catch-22 situations come with the territory. Although you've just lost your job, you've waited for three hours to get to this desk, and someone has just given you an absurd hoop to jump, you must keep your cool and do what they say. If they want you to be willing to accept shift work as a corporate vice president, agree to it. Remember that to argue or thwart the process in any way may affect your eligibility.

Approach the process as if the person behind the desk has numerous bags of money under the desk. If you are calm and pleasant and follow all the rules someone will give you one of the bags. The people at the unemployment office who have direct contact with the public have very little power to do anything except slow down your claim. If you abuse them, you may be waiting a long time before you see your first check.

What's a government office without a few forms? Every state has a form all its own. As an example, an unemployment compensation form for the state of Ohio appears on the next page.

The form you file will likely have a number of questions relating to your reasons for applying, previous claims, and general personal data. As you complete the form, there are several things to remember:

This IS a test. You do have to come up with the right answers. If they want you to agree to work weekends, agree to it, even if you are a bank teller. This doesn't mean you necessarily have to accept a job that requires weekend work. It simply means you are *willing* to accept one. The distinction is enough to stall your claim or make it sail through the bureaucracy.

Don't lie. They do check. Unemployment forms are not like tax returns. They don't check a random few, they check them all. This is because your employer must agree with you that you were not fired for some sort of misconduct. In that respect, your employer will be asked some of the same questions you are asked. If your answers don't agree, your claim may be denied. In the event your employer responds in a way that causes your claim to be denied, you can and should file an appeal, especially if your answers were right in the first place.

If you're confused, ask someone. You may get more than one answer to the same question, but if you're confused, you're better off being able to say, "Gee, so-and-so in the unemployment office told me to answer that way" than to guess on your own and make a mistake.

If all else fails, find a construction worker. Finally, if all else fails and the forms have you completely confused, look around the unemployment office and find someone who

APPLICATION FOR DETERMINATION OF BENEFIT RIGHTS AND WORK REGISTRATION

CLAIMANT: Do not complete the shaded items.

1. Social Security Account Number	23.	24.	25. Previous Benfit Year	26. Application Date

23.
1 ☐ M
2 ☐ F

24.
1 ☐ W   4 ☐ I
2 ☐ B   5 ☐ A/PI
3 ☐ H   6 ☐ NA

27. Benefit Year Begins

To Claimant: READ and COMPLETE ITEMS 1 through 21. PLEASE PRINT! DO NOT COMPLETE THE SHADED ITEMS.

28. Benefit Year Ends

2. Name _____ (last) _____ (first) _____ (middle initial) _____ (_____) (former last name)

29. Return:

3. Address _____ (number) _____ (street)

_____ (city) _____ (state) _____ (zip code) _____ (county)

30. Claim Type:
1 ☐ Regular Ohio   5 ☐ UCX
2 ☐ CWC   6 ☐ UCFE
3 ☐ TRA   7 ☐ DUA
4 ☐ Seasonal   8 ☐ School

4. Telephone Number
(_____)
(area code)

5. Birthdate
(month) (day) (year)

6. Age

31. Disallow
a. 1 ☐ Less than 20 weeks
   2 ☐ BYE not expired
   3 ☐ App. Improp. filed
   4 ☐ Insufficient wages
   5 ☐ App. withdrawn
   6 ☐ Not unemployed

7. Circle the highest grade you completed in school. If you graduated, circle "GRAD" instead of "4."

GRADE SCHOOL	HIGH SCHOOL	COLLEGE
C 1 2 3 4 5 6 7 8	1 2 3 4 GRAD	1 2 3 4 GRAD
0 1 2 3 4 5 6 7 8	9 10 11 12 13	14 15 16 17 18

8. What is your usual trade or occupation?

9. If you worked less than full-time during any of the past four calendar weeks, enter your gross earnings in the blocks below. DO NOT MAKE AN ENTRY FOR ANY WEEK IN WHICH YOU DID NOT WORK OR YOU WORKED FULL-TIME.

Last Week	Two Weeks Ago	Three Weeks Ago	Four Weeks Ago
$	$	$	$

10. Have you filed for unemployment benefits in Ohio or any other state during the last fifty-two weeks?
☐ YES ☐ NO

b. Send 465
1 ☐ D.P.
2 ☐ L.O.

32. Prior Partials
1 ☐ Yes
2 ☐ No

11. When employed, are you the principal wage or salary earner in your family or household? .... ☐ YES ☐ NO

12. Are you or have you been an officer of a corporation, or did you own or operate a business within the past 18 months? .... ☐ YES ☐ NO

13. Are you a citizen of the United States? .... ☐ YES ☐ NO
If "NO," what authorization did you obtain to perform employment in the United States?

14. Are you receiving or have you applied for any type of retirement or pension? .... ☐ YES ☐ NO
If "YES," state the gross amount of the pension $_____ for each ☐ MONTH ☐ OTHER (specify) _____
What is the source of the pension(s)? _____

33. Report Day
1 ☐ MON
2 ☐ TUE
3 ☐ WED
4 ☐ THUR
5 ☐ FRI

34. Report Cycle
1 ☐   5 ☐
2 ☐   6 ☐
3 ☐   7 ☐
4 ☐   8 ☐

35. PWE
    YES NO
1 ☐ 2 ☐

36. ETO
1 ☐ A   3 ☐ C _____
2 ☐ B   4 ☐ D _____

15a. Enter the name and PAYROLL address of all employers for whom you have worked DURING your LAST 6 weeks of employment. Include Ohio, out-of-state, federal civilian employment and active military service. If you have any documents given to you by your employer(s), copy their names and addresses from such forms. Failure to list all employment may affect your rights and benefits. ON YOUR NEXT REPORT TO THIS OFFICE, BRING VERIFICATION OF EMPLOYMENT LISTED SUCH AS CHECK STUBS, PAYROLL SLIPS, AND W-2 INCOME TAX FORMS.

Most Recent Employer _____

Number Weeks Worked _____   Gross Average Weekly Wage $_____

Number and Street _____

Plant or Store Number _____   Clock/Badge Number _____

City _____   State _____

County Where Employed _____   Zip Code _____

Reason for Separation _____

37. FIPS Code
(state) (county)

38. Education

39. Dependency
☐ A ☐ B ☐ C

42.
Employer Number

VERIFICATION
1 ☐ L.O.W.   ☐ Yes   ☐ Pay Stubs
2 ☐ Other   seq. UC-425 ☐ Other _____
3 ☐ Labor Dis.   (specify)

Date Hired
(month) (day) (year)

Last Day Worked
(month) (day) (year)

DO YOU EXPECT TO RETURN TO WORK FOR THE ABOVE EMPLOYER? ☐ YES ☐ NO If "YES," when? _____

40. ISSUES
01 ☐ Refer to Examiner
02 ☐ R/Sep-no. 410D/Q's _____
03 ☐ Corp/Citizen/Pension
04 ☐ Dependency
05 ☐ Earnings/Income
06 ☐ Code/Title
07 ☐ Ver. Wgs-Emp. No. _____
08 ☐ Alternate Base Period
09 ☐ Emp. Liability
10 ☐ Verify Spouse SS No.
11 ☐ Verify Claimant SS No.
12 ☐ Able/Avail./ASW
13 ☐ Break
14 ☐ Other _____

15b. Have your received or are you expecting a decision from OBES on your reason for separation from any of the employers you have listed on your application? .... ☐ YES ☐ NO

15c. The following question will be used for statistical purposes only. It is requested on a voluntary basis and refusal to provide the information will not subject you to any adverse treatment. The information will be kept confidential and will not affect determinations made in regard to your right to claim benefits.
Are you Handicapped as defined in Section 504 of the Rehabilitation Act of 1973? .... ☐ YES ☐ NO
The definition of handicapped is as follows: "A person is handicapped if he or she has a physical or mental impairment which substantially limits one or more major life activities; has a record of such impairment; or is regarded as having such impairment".

16. a. Are you required to pay child support to a court or a child support enforcement agency? ☐ YES ☐ NO
    b. If "YES," enter name and address of agency

(name) (county)

ADDRESS (street) (city) (state) (zip code)

41. Local Office Number

IF YOU WORKED FOR OTHER EMPLOYERS DURING YOUR LAST 6 WEEKS OF EMPLOYMENT, OR IF DURING THE LAST 18 MONTHS HAD OUT-OF-STATE, FEDERAL CIVILIAN OR MILITARY EMPLOYMENT, CHECK THE BLOCK ☐ AND ASK FOR AN ADDITIONAL FORM.
UC-401N (R 8-90) BES 0334 55313   IMPORTANT — COMPLETE OTHER SIDE

(continued)

Unemployment compensation form for the state of Ohio.

17. **DEPENDENCY INFORMATION:** If you have dependents as defined in the law, your weekly benefit amount may be increased. The maximum number of dependents that can increase your weekly amount is three. A dependent is defined as :

   a. **YOUR SPOUSE — LEGALLY MARRIED WIFE OR HUSBAND,** living with you and for whom you provided more than one-half the cost of support during the past ninety days, or for the duration of the marital relationship if it existed for less than ninety days, and during this period the person claimed as a dependent did not have an average weekly income in excess of twenty-five percent of your base period average weekly wage; and

   b. **YOUR CHILD, STEPCHILD, OR ADOPTED CHILD,** under eighteen years of age or, if eighteen or over and unable to work because of permanent physical or mental disability, for whom you provided more than one-half the cost of support during the past ninety days, or for the duration of the parental relationship if it existed for less than ninety days.

   If you claim dependents, you may be required to submit documentary evidence (marriage, certificate, birth certificate(s), medical report, or evidence of support payments to verify your claim.

18. ☐ **IF YOU ARE NOT CLAIMING DEPENDENTS AS DEFINED ABOVE, PLACE AN "X", IN THE BLOCK AND TAKE THIS APPLICATION TO THE CLAIMS COUNTER. DO NOT COMPLETE ITEMS 19, 20 or 21.**

19. Has your spouse applied for unemployment benefits during the past year? .... ☐ YES ☐ NO

   If "Yes"   a. In which local office? _____
                        Spouse's Social Security
                        b. Account Number _____

20. DEPENDENT SPOUSE (wife or husband), COMPLETE ITEMS 20a THROUGH 20e <u>ONLY</u> IF YOU WISH TO CLAIM YOUR SPOUSE AS A DEPENDENT. *(SEE LAW REQUIREMENTS IN ITEM 17a ABOVE.)*

   a. Spouse's name _____

   b. Are you living together? .... ☐ YES ☐ NO
       If "NO," explain: _____

   c. Has your spouse been employed within the last ninety days .... ☐ YES ☐ NO
       If "YES", (1) List his or her gross average weekly wage $ _____
                (2) Name and address of his or her employer _____
                                NAME

                                ADDRESS   (street)   (city)   (state)   (zip code)

                (3) Was your spouse continuously employed during the ninety days? .... ☐ YES ☐ NO
                (4) If "NO," how many weeks did he or she work? _____

   d. Did your spouse have income from any other source during the last ninety days? .... ☐ YES ☐ NO
       If "YES," enter source of such income _____ and the gross average weekly amount $ _____

   e. If you have been married for a period of less than ninety days, enter the date of your marriage. _____

21. **DEPENDENT CHILDREN, COMPLETE ITEMS 21a THROUGH 21g ONLY IF YOU HAVE CHILDREN YOU WISH TO CLAIM AS DEPENDENTS.** *(SEE LAW REQUIREMENTS IN ITEM 17b ABOVE.)*

a. Names of your children, step children or adopted children for whom you provided more than one-half of the support.		b. What relation is this child to you? (i.e., son, stepson, adopted son, etc.)	c. Do they live with you?	d. Date of birth mo. day year	e. Name of school child(ren) attend
First	*Last*				
First	*Last*				
First	*Last*				

   f. Are you living with your spouse? .... ☐ YES ☐ NO
   g. For each of your children listed in item 21a who is eighteen years of age or older, indicate whether such child has a permanent physical or mental handicap, and whether or not this prevents the child from working.

22a. **PRIVACY ACT STATEMENT:** The Privacy Act of 1974 requires you be advised of this statement because you are being asked to furnish your social security account number on the claim forms given to you. Your social security account number is solicited under the authority of the Internal Revenue Code of 1954 (26 U.S.C. 85.6011(a), 6050B, and 6109(a)). Disclosure of your social security account number for this purpose is MANDATORY, and must be entered on the forms you submit to claim unemployment compensation.

Your social security account number will be used to report your unemployment compensation to the Internal Revenue Service as income that is potentially taxable: it will also be used as a record index for processing your claim, for statistical purposes, and to verify your eligibility for unemployment compensation and other public assistance benefits. SHOULD YOU DECLINE TO DISCLOSE YOUR SOCIAL SECURITY ACCOUNT NUMBER, YOUR CLAIM FOR UNEMPLOYMENT COMPENSATION WILL NOT BE PROCESSED.

   b. **CERTIFICATION:** I certify that I am unemployed and I hereby register for work and make application for determination of my benefit rights. Further, I certify that the statements, made by me, on both sides of this form are true and correct and that during the past ninety days, or for the duration of the marital or parental relationship if it existed less than ninety days, I provided more than one-half the cost of support of the dependent(s) listed on this application. I know the law provides penalties for false statements to obtain benefits.

   Signature of applicant .... Date ....

ID: ☐ DR;   ☐ W-2;   ☐ CC;   ☐ _____ Signature of claims taker ....

Unemployment compensation form for the state of Ohio (continued).

looks like a construction worker. Many people who work in construction deal with seasonal employment shifts that put them out of work from time to time. After one or two times through the system, they have learned how to answer the questions and save themselves time and headaches.

If you're not sure how your employer will respond, ask for a fact-finding interview. Remember, unemployment compensation is available to people who are out of work through no fault of their own. If you were fired or laid off but committed no misconduct, you are generally eligible for unemployment. However, if your employer disagrees, he or she may tell the unemployment office that you were fired "for cause," which would invalidate your claim. If the circumstances under which you left were strained, or if you think your employer would try to have your claim denied for any reason, ask for a fact-finding interview *when you turn in your original claim*. A fact-finding interview will require your employer to appear with you at an informal meeting during which a representative from the unemployment office will try to determine the actual circumstances of your departure. This can be an important step and a relatively painless way to avoid a potentially lengthy appeal process.

Appeal a Bad Decision

Crazy as it may sound, you may do everything right and still find that your claim has been denied. If this happens, the most important thing to remember is the old Yogi Berra adage, "It ain't over 'til it's over." In most states, that's true for at least half the people whose claims are initially refused. In other words, if your claim is denied, your chances are 50-50 of having the denial overturned by your appeal.

An appeal will, of course, require another form and another

trip to the office. The hundreds or even thousands of dollars you can receive on appeal are worth the trip. Appealing a decision is a little like deciding to appear in traffic court, only your chances of winning are better.

When you receive notice that your benefits have been denied, a reason for the denial will appear on the form. Basically, these reasons fall into two categories: Either the unemployment office believes you do not fit their criteria for compensation, or your former employer responded in a way that refuted your responses. In fact, even if your claim is initially granted, your former employer can appeal the claim. In this case, you will be required to attend a hearing, just as if you had filed an appeal yourself.

Similar to a traffic court hearing, once you appeal you will be assigned a date on which you are expected to appear for a hearing. And, like a traffic court hearing, the more information you can bring to support your case, the better your chances of having the ruling go in your favor. Witnesses, signed letters that support your position, even a written severance agreement between you and your former employer can help you win your case. The examples below show some of the reasons your claim may be denied and give you ideas of the kind of evidence you should bring with you to your hearing.

> *Your employer says you were fired for miscon-duct.* Assuming your employer's statement isn't true, the burden of proof is on him or her. Most states have fairly strict guidelines of what they consider to be misconduct. However, if you and your former employer show up to the hearing alone, it may come down to his word against yours. In this situation, you may want to get a former co-worker to come with you and testify that you were not fired for misconduct. A signed letter will also help. A written severance agreement, detailing the reasons for your termination, will help as well. In most cases, though, unless your former

employer is actually out to defraud the unemployment system, he or she will not realize that "misconduct" has a very strict definition according to the state. If your employer believes that a personality conflict counts as misconduct, you've most likely already won.

The state doesn't think you are willing to accept suitable work. In other words, on the original form you got one of the answers wrong. You may have said you were unwilling to work second shift or that you would only accept a job with a starting salary well above what you were making. In this case, you may simply need to justify your answer to the state's representative at the hearing. If, for example, you were a bank teller and no banks in your area are open on Saturday, you can probably make a case for refusing to work on Saturdays.

Your employer made it impossible for you to stay, and the state believes you quit without just cause. Sometimes, an employer can make an employment situation unbearable. You may wish he or she would lay you off and give you some sort of reasonable severance pay. For example, suppose a junior architect is hired with the understanding that he will generally not have to work much overtime, but, if he does, he will be paid for it. After a few months on the job, his deadlines and responsibilities mount, and his hours increase dramatically. If he quits and his claim is denied, he can make a strong case that he had just cause for quitting, especially if he can bring along a co-worker to attest to the long hours and lack of overtime pay. Remember, you can quit and still receive benefits, as long as you can justify leaving. Your justification on your original claim form may not have been clear enough, and the hearing will be your chance to clarify your position.

Most importantly, before you attend your appeal hearing, make sure you are prepared. You might want to rehearse what you will say with a friend and try to think of questions they may ask you. Be sure you have a coherent argument and plan to introduce at least one piece of evidence (a letter, witness, severance agreement) in your favor.

Witnesses can definitely help your case. If a witness you'd like to call still works for your former employer, however, and is concerned about appearing for you, you can ask the unemployment office to subpoena him or her. The office will comply with all reasonable requests to subpoena someone who can help your case.

Before your appeal hearing, if you are concerned that you will have difficulty making your case, you may want to look to some readily available sources for help. Depending on your financial situation and contacts in the community, you can use any one of these sources for help in developing your case:

Legal aid societies. Many cities have legal aid societies that provide legal advice at little or no charge. Given your current job situation, you may qualify for this low-cost service. Many legal aid societies have dealt with comparatively simple legal matters, such as unemployment compensation appeals. Lawyers who work for such an agency or donate their time to one can review your evidence and give you advice on how to present it or how to reinforce your case with other evidence.

Church and community groups. Many church and community groups have staff members or volunteers who can help with such events as unemployment hearings. If nothing else, you may be able to find someone who can help you rehearse and can attend the hearing with you to lend moral support. In addition, if you belong to a church, it's likely that they've helped other people in your situation. They may have some helpful ideas and advice.

Professional organizations. Although you may have some reluctance about letting your colleagues know you are out of a job, if you belong to a professional organization, you have access to a number of people who can help you. The organization may have access to inexpensive legal counsel that you can use to help reinforce your case.

Talk with an attorney. Working with an attorney may be an expensive option that is not worth the investment for what you may gain. However, if you or someone in your family has dealt with an attorney on other matters, the attorney may be willing to give you low-cost advice, given your current employment situation. It's not necessary to have an attorney go with you to the hearing. As long as you've prepared a coherent case, which an attorney can help you do, you have a good chance of winning your appeal.

Know the Tax Laws

It shouldn't surprise you to know that unemployment compensation can be considered taxable income. However, the compensation you receive is taxable only if your income is above a specific limit. This limit may change as inflation affects people's salaries and as federal and state governments modify tax laws. You would be best advised to ask at the information desk at the unemployment office. Based on your income to date for the current year, as well as any other sources of income you may currently have, someone at the information desk should be able to tell you if your compensation will be taxed.

If your income for the year will be high enough that your unemployment compensation will be taxable, be aware that the government *does not* withhold taxes from your check the way an employer does. If you receive unemployment compensation for part of a year and your income for the remainder of the year puts you above the taxable limit, you will owe income taxes on the money you received from the unemployment system.

6 | Family Financial Security

Jane Bryant Quinn writes for *Newsweek* magazine. She contends, "In my business, if you've never been fired you haven't played for the biggest stakes. At a dinner once, I quizzed the table: Who had ever lost a job? Practically all of us, as it turned out. Me, twice. A TV producer I know, who has been fired by all three major networks (and is now back at work at one of them), framed his get-lost letters and hung them in the guest bathroom. On my own second time around, I bought a T-shirt. On the front it said, 'Yes, I was fired.' On the back, it said, 'Again.' "

People who have lost a job more than once become experts at the art of juggling financial responsibilities. If this is your first time, your reactions can range from bravado ("Why do I need to clip coupons? I'll have another job *long* before my severance pay runs out") to panic ("Oh, my God, we'll lose the house!"). In truth, neither reaction makes much sense if you're out of a job. With a little creativity, you can juggle your responsibilities and, depending on how much you may have in savings, buy yourself at least a year, which is more than enough time for most people out of work.

Regardless of the severance agreement you negotiate, financial concerns inevitably surface when you're out of work. The fact that there may be other people depending on your income, such as a spouse, children, or aging parents, compounds your concern. The easiest way to deal with your immediate concerns is to get a clear picture of your current financial situation. If you aren't an organized person when it comes to finances, losing your job will certainly help you focus more on what you earn, how you spend your money, and how you control both. It may seem like learning the hard way, but many people say that losing a job has helped them focus on saving more money, wasting less, and reducing or eliminating debt.

The first step in gaining control is to put it on paper, making a budget. If you already keep reasonable account of your income, debts, and expenses, a large part of the process is already finished. In that case, you need only prioritize your debts and expenses to ensure that the most important bills are paid first, things that can be put off are delayed, and you don't severely damage your credit rating in the process.

For many people, the idea of doing a budget is about as appealing as having a root canal. You probably don't lie awake nights thinking, "Gee, I ought to do a budget." More likely, you know "approximately" where the money goes. The important part about being laid off is that you need to know where *all* of it goes. Because there may be no immediate end to your current situation, you need to conserve every resource. Financial planners say that when most people are asked to show how they spend their money, they are typically unable to account for at least 25 percent of their income. That kind of money *definitely* comes in handy when you're short one income.

The budgeting process itself is relatively simple. You make a list of everything you buy or owe and determine how much money you spend on each item. When you add your expenses, the total should be something less than or equal to your income. The problem is, if you have already read the chapter on unemployment compensation, you know that once your severance pay runs out, your income will be significantly less than it was when you were employed. And, unlike the federal government, *your* budget has to balance.

Obviously, something has to go. The point of the rest of this chapter is to help you decide what to keep in the budget, what to delay, and what to delete altogether. The key to a successful unemployment budget is to *plan* to be out of work for at least nine months to a year. According to national averages, you probably won't be looking that long, however, your plan should give you more time than you'll need so that you can ensure your family's financial security.

START WITH A LIST

If you are one of those organized people, boot up your home computer, access your budget spreadsheet, and print a copy of your current budget. If you're a little more normal than that, make a list similar to the one shown here:

Spending

Savings	*Expenses*
Future education	Rent
Vacation	Groceries
Retirement	Medical costs
Future home	Transportation
New car	−gas
Christmas	−maintenance
	Insurance
	−house/renter
	−life

Spending

Savings

Expenses

–car

–medical

Taxes

–real estate

–federal

–state

Miscellaneous loans

–mortgage

–second mortgage

–consolidation

–charge cards

–car payment

–education loans

Alimony/child support

Child care/day care

Tuition

Charitable donations

Utilities

Other household expenses

–repairs

–cleaning service

–lawn/snow removal

Entertainment

Personal

–health club

–gifts

–clothing

Your list may not contain everything shown here, or it may have expenses this list doesn't include. Again, the important part of the process is to get as close as possible to knowing where *all* your money goes. Once you've created the list, look back over the last three or four months to determine how much you have been spending on each item. For some things, such as mortgage payments and car insurance, the amount will be easy to determine. Other items vary from month to month and are more difficult to track. Put down a number for every item, being as accurate as possible. Add the total to be sure that it corresponds fairly closely to the monthly income you were earning before you were unemployed.

ADD YOUR INCOME

Once you have the list of your expenses, determine what your income will be *without* your severance payments. If you are not receiving severance payments, this figure is the total of your income from any other sources plus your unemployment compensation.

If you are currently receiving severance payments, you should still calculate your income *without* severance payments. Although many people do start new jobs before their severance period ends, that is not always the case. If you get used to dealing with a reduced income now, the transition will be that much easier. In addition, this strategy forces you to face your finanical situation squarely, reducing the shock if your severance pay runs out, and giving you a great deal of added incentive for your job search.

As you develop your budget, then, you need to plan for the worst-case scenario. In other words, get used to living on unemployment *now* rather than later. If you are receiving severance pay and haven't yet applied for unemployment compensation, you should read Chapter 5 and be aware of the amount you are likely to receive if you eventually do apply. In many cases, you will receive approximately $800 per month if you have no dependents, and somewhere near $1200 if you have one or more dependents. Remember, as you build your budget, don't assume you can spend your entire severance check each month. Rather, you should try to get as close to a true unemployment budget as you possibly can so that when your severance pay does run out, it's not a shock, and so that you can learn to save as much of your severance pay as possible.

Even if you honestly believe that you will find another job before your severance pay runs out, be conservative anyway. Assume that you will not find another job soon enough and start living on less now. Then if you do find another job quickly, the severance pay you have left can become additional savings for you and your family.

WHAT TO CHOOSE

Once you calculate your new income and compare it against your old expenses, you'll realize a significant disparity. The rest of the budgeting process involves choosing what to pay and what to delay. There are a number of important factors that should enter into your decisions as you look down the list. The most important thing to remember is that, as long as you already have a reasonable financial record, most of the companies or agencies you owe money to will be willing to work with you on paying what you owe. If you contact them before the situation gets out of control, explain the situation, and offer to work out a reasonable plan for payment, your creditors will tend to appreciate your initiative and try to work with you. Above all, be creative.

Here are some things to consider as you look at your list:

Savings

You probably won't be able to contribute to savings, and may even be forced to use some of your savings to get you through your unemployment. If you do start spending your savings, keep track of how much you spend. You will "owe" yourself that money when you start your new position. Keeping track of the bill will give you added incentive to increase your savings when you start back to work.

If you do have to start spending your savings, don't touch your retirement savings. This is important because most retirement plans are tax-deferred, meaning that you may have to pay a substantial penalty in addition to the taxes that were deferred when you set up your retirement account. Your best bet is to ignore your retirement savings altogether, using them only when you are absolutely certain you have no other choice.

Rent

If you don't own your own home, one of the more difficult payments to negotiate will be your rent payment. Depending on your situation and relationship with your landlord, you may be able to negotiate some reduced payment plan. The cost of evicting a tenant may be a point in your favor if you try to negotiate a temporary reduction in your rent. If the economy is not strong and your landlord is concerned about vacant units, he or she may accept your reduced rent rather than have another vacant unit.

Insurance

Insurance is critical to your family's security. Under no circumstances should you decide to go without insurance altogether, whatever your reasoning. You may be thinking, "What are the odds something will happen in the few months I'll be out of work?" Don't risk it. If you think you have financial concerns now, imagine what it would be like if you were out of work *and* your car was demolished in an accident for which you were not insured.

For health insurance, if you were not able to negotiate continued health benefits as part of your severance package, ask your former employer if you can pay to remain on the policy. In most cases, the cost will be much less than you would have to pay to buy a policy as an individual. As mentioned in Chapter 2, federal law requires most employers to allow terminated employees to purchase health benefits at the employer's group rate. According to a statute of the Consolidated Omnibus Budget Reconciliation Act (COBRA) of 1986, your employer may be required to allow you to participate in the company's group health plan for up to 18 months from the date of your termination. A few criteria may apply, but in general, if your employer has more than 20 employees and you were not terminated for misconduct, you should be eligible to continue to receive health benefits for which you pay the group rate. Your employer's human resources manager should have information on COBRA laws and their impact on your situation.

Life insurance is equally critical to your family's welfare. If you no longer have coverage from your former employer, buy the least expensive term policy you can find. Whether you are out of a job or not, term life insurance is always a better buy than a whole life policy. Shop around to find an inexpensive policy. You may think you can do without for now. Your family would think otherwise if something happens to you while you are out of work.

Utilities

Looking for a job without a telephone is like trying to dig a trench with a soup spoon. Some things you just cannot do without.

Electricity and gas are also on the critical list. However, you may be able to work out some sort of payment plan with the utility company. Usually, you have to be delinquent for a number of months before they'll consider cutting off your electricity or gas. You shouldn't push your luck, though. Don't wait several months before talking with a utility company about your situation. The sooner you approach them, the more cooperative they're likely to be.

Other utilities, such as water or sewer assessments, are easier to deal with because they are paid on a quarterly or semi-annual basis. These bills are also generally small compared to your other obligations. You may even have another job before you have to worry about paying these bills. Again, call the water department or other agency if you think it will be a problem.

Groceries and Household Expenses

This category is fairly obvious. You can't do without groceries, but you can be stubbornly cost-conscious. You remember how to do it: You did it right after college or when you were first married. Relearn the art of comparison shopping. Use comparison tactics for everything, for even the smallest can of beans. Clip coupons and buy generics. Make a list *before* you go, and don't buy anything not on the list.

When shopping for groceries, buy as few prepared foods (TV dinners or other frozen meals) as possible. Ounce per ounce, prepared foods cost significantly more than foods you prepare yourself. While you're looking for work, you'll have plenty of time to prepare your own meals every night.

Finally, as trivial as it may sound, *don't buy anything you don't need*. It may make you feel better to buy an expensive bottle of wine, but it won't help in the long run. If you're careful, you can cut your grocery bill by 20 or 25 percent, money you definitely need right now.

Loan Payments

When you make your list of expenses, "mortgage loan" probably tops the list. If you're like most people, you shopped for a house using one of the old rules of thumb about making sure your mortgage payment was no more than a certain percentage of your gross monthly income. Now that your gross monthly income has been drastically reduced, your mortgage payment may seem like an enormous bill.

The most important thing to remember about dealing with lenders is that they don't want to foreclose any more than you want them to, especially if you have had a good record with them so far. Foreclosing on your house, especially if the economy is in bad shape, may not even net the bank enough money to cover what you owe. On the other hand, if they can work out a reasonable payment plan with you, both parties will be much better off in the long run.

As with any money you owe, your best bet is to show initiative and make the first move. Get an appointment to talk with your loan officer. When you meet, calmly explain your situation and provide a proposal for paying what you can. In many instances, a bank will allow you to pay only the interest on your mortgage for a period of time. This can drastically reduce your payments while ensuring that the bank is still receiving some return on its investment.

If you have a second mortgage loan, you may be able to work out a similar payment scheme. Most importantly, don't wait until the situation is out of control. Don't assume you'll have a job in three months and that it won't be a problem to be a few months delinquent on your loan. Not only will that make it extremely difficult to negotiate some other payment scheme if you're still out of work after three months, it can also significantly damage your credit rating.

Some other loans and thoughts on how to handle them are:

Credit cards. If you have large credit card balances, you'll need to postpone payments on them as long as possible. Having cash on hand is far more important than your credit rating right now. If you have money in savings, don't use it to pay credit card balances. Even though the interest rate you are paying on credit card balances far outweighs any interest you may be earning on any kind of savings or investment plan, you need to preserve cash. The goal with credit cards is to pay as little as possible on each balance.

Assuming you have a reasonable credit rating, you can write to the manager of the credit department of the bank that issued the credit card. Explain that you recently lost your job, highlighting the fact that your credit rating has always been good, and ask for his or her consideration for a short period. If you offer to make monthly "good faith" payments ($5 or $10) and keep your word, the bank will likely work with you. Again, if you take the first step, any creditor will appreciate your initiative and be more likely to work with you.

Most importantly, if you have outstanding balances on one or more credit cards, take a pair of scissors and cut up all but one card. The card you keep should be a nationally recognized card (VISA, MasterCard, Discover, American Express, AT&T Universal Card) with the lowest balance. Use that card *only* for emergencies. Actually, this is good advice even if you are not unemployed. When you do start your next job, your *first* financial goal should be to rid yourself of high-interest credit card balances forever.

Consolidation loans. As with credit cards, write to the company holding your loan and set up a payment plan. Some payment is better than no payment at this point. Remember, though, hanging on to your cash is more important than maintaining an impeccable credit rating at this point.

Car payments. If you're part of a two-person working family, you may actually be able to do without one car. As strange as the idea may seem, you can get up every morning and drive your spouse to work, or he or she can try to find a car pool. Then you can sell one car and use the remaining one as you search for a new position. This is especially helpful advice if your car payment is large. As hard as it may be to part with an expensive car you waited years to buy, you really don't need that outrageous payment right now.

If you can't do without and have to make car payments, use the same strategy you're using with other loan payments. Take the initiative to work out a payment plan with the bank or finance company.

Transportation Costs

Because you'll be interviewing, you have to have reliable transportation. Beyond the cost of the loan, you'll have to pay for gas, repairs, and preventative maintenance for your car. At this point, do whatever maintenance you can do on your own. Delay anything expensive (15,000-mile checkups) and do the things that can have the most impact. Most car experts believe that changing your oil often is the cheapest, most important car maintenance item. It's also relatively simple to do on your own. Any repairs that do not cause a safety problem should be postponed.

Taxes

It's been said more than once that the only things certain in life are death and taxes. When you're out of work, it may feel like death, but you still have to pay taxes. The key is, you may be able to avoid paying them on time, allowing you to preserve cash for more immediate personal concerns. Before you make any decisions on taxes, though, you should consult the IRS, a tax attorney, an expert on tax returns, or some other professional to determine all your options.

To say the least, local, state, and federal governments tend to be somewhat adamant that you pay your taxes. However, you may be surprised to know that you do have a few options that you may want to take advantage of. You should remember that some of these options may involve penalties of some sort, but your goal can be to delay payments as long as possible, allowing you to conserve precious cash. Some ideas for dealing with taxes are:

> *Real estate taxes.* Real estate taxes are generally paid twice per year. If you are lucky and the timing of your layoff is right, you may not have to worry about real estate taxes for several months. If your taxes are due soon, though, you'll have to come up with an appropriate plan. Because eviction and auction sales are difficult legal processes that can be expensive and time-consuming, county governments tend to avoid them at all costs. Some counties don't even consider your real estate taxes delinquent until you have gone one year without paying a tax bill. After that, it can take up to a year for you to be placed on a list of properties considered delinquent before the legal maneuverings involved in an auction sale can even begin. The bottom line on real estate taxes is that it is highly unlikely that you will be out of work long enough to make you delinquent on your real estate taxes.

> On the other hand, you shouldn't take this situation as an invitation to disregard your real estate tax bill. As with any other obligation, you should contact the real estate tax office in your area, explain your situation, and work out a payment plan. Again, because the government would rather avoid

auction sales at all costs, you'll likely find that they are more than willing to work with you.

Income tax. There are two concerns with income taxes that you need to be aware of if you are unemployed. The first is that unemployment compensation may be taxable. Because the unemployment office will not withhold federal or state taxes from your compensation, you need to be aware of any possible tax liabilities. In general, you will need to file a quarterly estimated tax form (and pay any taxes due) for your unemployment compensation *if you meet certain criteria*. In other words, if your income for the year is above a certain level, your unemployment benefits will be taxable and you will have to pay quarterly taxes to avoid penalties. The IRS suggests that you contact them to discuss your situation and determine if you must file quarterly taxes. Your best bet in this situation is to contact the IRS or state government to determine what, if anything, you should be paying on a quarterly estimated basis. Given the fact that unemployment compensation is generally fairly low, the taxes you owe will not likely be exorbitant, and you should pay them right away to avoid penalties later.

The second important concern about income taxes is likely to cause you more problems. If you are unemployed around April 15 and you owe a significant amount of income taxes, you may not have the money to pay them right now. Because the IRS tends to be a stickler when it comes to you owing them money, this can be a delicate situation. According to the IRS information line, the worst thing you can do is ignore the April 15 deadline altogether. You should prepare your tax form as accurately as possible and calculate the amount of tax you currently owe. Do the same for state taxes. You should file your return on time, paying all that you can possibly afford to pay, and you will automatically begin paying interest and penalties on the amount you still owe. However, in the words of one IRS telephone assistor, they will not "take your firstborn or your car or something." Instead, you will be notified that you are delinquent and that you now owe the balance plus interest and penalties. When you receive this notice, you may want to call the IRS, explain your situation, and ask to work out a payment plan. It's not the IRS's policy to devise payment plans for taxpayers. However, they're more likely to resort to some type of plan than to try to repossess your car if they think they can get the money faster.

Whatever your situation, if you have questions, find someone who can help. Use the IRS toll-free number (1-800-829-1040) to call and get more information. Talk to friends or family members who may have experienced similar problems. Ask around at your church, community group, or professional organization to see if anyone has expertise in preparing tax returns. Above all else, try to work within the government's regulations whenever possible. Don't simply ignore deadlines. As with any debt, your cooperation will go a long way toward easing the situation for you.

Alimony or Child Support

If you are making monthly alimony or child support payments, your payments are based on your salary *before* you were laid off. There may not be any provision in your divorce decree to deal with drastic changes to your income. Rather than let your payments lapse or try to negotiate with your former spouse, you should consult the attorney who handled your divorce proceedings.

Although laws may vary from state to state, you will likely have to work through the court to make any changes to your current payments. Because being out of work involves numerous

financial choices, you'll probably want to put child support payments ahead of any alimony obligations you may have. However,
because you are legally bound to pay both if that's what your
divorce decree included, you may not be able to negotiate exactly
what you need. This is one area in which you may have very little
flexibility. In addition, your options may be limited by the relationship between you and your former spouse.

Child Care or Day Care

It's not as easy as it sounds. One of you is out of work, the kids
can just stay home with him or her. This can save you hundreds
of dollars per month. You do need to realize that you still have
a full-time job (looking for another job) and that child care issues
will still arise. You won't be able to afford your usual child care
every day. However, there will be days when you will be interviewing and will need someone to stay with the kids.

Because of your situation, friends, family, and neighbors can
likely be counted on to help. Your usual day care center may
also offer drop-in service for those days that you'll be out interviewing. You can even try to schedule all your interviews and
meetings for one or two days every week. In general, however,
this will be one area that offers you the good potential for saving
money.

Tuition

Depending on whether you are dealing with a private grammar
school or a large university, tuition bills can be a significant
problem. If you have one or more children attending college,
call the financial aid office and explain your situation. Depending
on the size of the school, they may be able to help you apply for
loans or grants, depending on your son's or daughter's academic

standing. One parent discovered that a large state university had a fund to provide interest-free loans to students who were also scholarship recipients. Because his daughter had received a small scholarship earlier in her academic career, the university was able to grant her an interest-free loan that paid a large portion of her tutition. Financial aid offices can often be more creative than you would imagine, especially if your son or daughter has a reasonable academic record.

Small private colleges and private or parochial elementary or preparatory schools may be able to help you set up a payment plan. Depending on your prospects for a new job, though, this may be the time to talk with your children about the possibility of completing their education at a less expensive school.

Charitable Donations

Obviously when you're worried about where your next paycheck will come from, it's difficult to be concerned about the plight of others. Charitable donations are probably the first thing on your list that you'll immediately delete. You do have good reason for putting your family's security ahead of donations you may normally make. However, there are a couple of things you can do to ensure that you still share your valuable resources.

When you're out of work, there are only so many hours in a day you can stuff resumés into envelopes or go on interviews. You'll likely have time that you can use, although you'll have no idea how long that will be the case. One of the best ways to deal with the anxiety too much time produces is to volunteer, even if only for a few hours per week. Not only will volunteering help you deal with the open-ended anxiety of being out of work, it will also help you feel less isolated and more connected to other people. All the while, you'll still be fulfilling your community obligations, even if you can no longer do it financially.

Most important, when you do find another job, don't forget

to share your good fortune. Resume your donations and add additional funds if you can from time to time.

Entertainment and Personal Expenses

You'll be able to cut large portions of this part of your budget. You'll quickly begin to realize that one movie for two people can pay for groceries for a day for two people. You'll start to realize that there are tradeoffs with every dime you may think of spending.

On the other hand, some forms of inexpensive entertainment will help alleviate the boredom and anxiety. Rent a movie, go to an art museum on the day they have free admission, take the kids to any one of a number of free museums or historical exhibits.

Other personal expenses, such as dry cleaning or health club memberships can be reduced or eliminated altogether. Tape an exercise program from public television instead. If you press it carefully, a good suit can go through 10 or 15 wearings without being dry cleaned.

Gifts can be a problem when money is tight. Give family members a gift certificate for free baby-sitting or other services. They'll appreciate it more than you know, and they'll certainly understand, given your situation.

THE WORLD'S GREATEST CHEAPSKATE

Once you've decided on a budget, you and everyone in your family need to understand the budget and commit yourselves to staying within its constraints. If you can, force yourself to think of your severance pay as a bonus. In other words, stretch your severance pay as much as possible. Don't touch it at all if you can scrape by on your spouse's salary. Or use only $200 to $400 per week of your severance pay, roughly the amount you'll get from the unemployment office if your severance pay runs out before you start a new job.

The key to living on an unemployment budget is to be the world's greatest cheapskate. Don't make any purchases, from the smallest can of corn to a new pair of shoes, without asking yourself, "Is there any way I can get by without this?" If the answer is yes, don't buy it. If you're not used to a Spartan life style, this will be painful. Don't put off the pain until later; don't try to maintain a comfortable life style by eating through your savings or wasting any of your severance pay. You may be able to delay painful decisions, but that will make those decisions all the more difficult when you actually do have to face them.

If you received unused vacation pay from your employer in a lump-sum payment, don't touch any of it unless you have no other choice. If you do find another job quickly, unused vacation or severance pay can become a great bonus for your family, allowing you to reward them for surviving a difficult ordeal.

GETTING A LOAN TO HELP YOU THROUGH

Immediately after you are let go, if you are concerned about being able to weather an extended period of unemployment, you might want to apply for a loan to give you needed cash. Because any loan you assume will add to your debt and create another payment, you should apply for one only if you think you won't be able to survive at least nine months by using the tactics outlined in this chapter.

Applying for a loan when you don't have a job can be a tricky proposition, however. If you have a reasonable amount of equity in your home, your first choice should be to apply for a second mortgage loan or home equity loan. These loans will give you the best interest rate possible. If you have determined that you need a loan, call your former employer before you apply. The bank will ask him or her to complete a form, verifying the information you give them in your application. If you are covered under a severance agreement, your employer can technically state that you are still on his or her payroll and that your salary has not changed. You should not ask your employer to falsify your application, nor should he or she need to as long as you are still on the payroll under your severance agreement.

Rather than apply for a loan, you can ask to have your limit increased on one credit card. As mentioned in the section on credit cards in this chapter, you should avoid using credit cards except as a last resort. If you already have high balances on more than one card, you probably shouldn't try to increase your limit. The interest you are already paying each month offsets any cash-flow benefits you might obtain from increasing your limit. However, if your cards are paid off, they can provide a source of cash with postponable payments.

Borrowing Money from Friends or Family

Just the thought of going to mom or dad to ask for money to see you through can be a painful prospect. In general, if you can put together an unemployment budget that doesn't involve any kind of borrowing, you'll be in much better shape. Saddling yourself with a large amount of debt will put a great deal of pressure on you when you do find another job.

If you do have to borrow money, borrow it from a bank or other lending institution if possible before asking friends or family. At last resort, however, you may have to ask someone close to you to help you through a difficult time. If you ask or they offer, be sure you put everything in writing. It may sound odd, but the best way to preserve a good friendship or family relationship is to keep money out of it.

If your parents offer you money to help you through and you decide to accept their offer, be firm in telling them you plan to pay it back, then write them a letter telling them how you will pay it back. Your payment plan should start as soon as you find another job and should include regular monthly payments as if you owed money to any financial institution. Don't let them talk you out of it, and don't assume you'll pay them back "when you can." More family rifts have been created over money than anyone cares to count.

7 | Surviving Up to a Year Without an Income

Now that you know how to review your family's finances, this chapter shows two actual budget worksheets for a two-income family and a single-income family. These provide good examples of how you can survive for a year after losing one income.

Note that both families have *some* money in savings to begin with. Most financial planning experts agree that individuals should have at least three months' income in savings at all times in case of emergencies. Neither family in these examples, however, has this much in savings. As in the second example, if you haven't been saving, you may have to consider borrowing money to help you through your unemployment period. As mentioned before, however, borrowing should always be a last resort.

One important note: Don't forget that severance pay packages may have an impact on unemployment benefits. You should contact your local unemployment office if you have questions about the relationship between severance pay and unemployment compensation.

THE TWO-INCOME FAMILY

The first example is for a two-income family that suddenly loses one income. Although the salary lost is the lesser of the two, the second income is not much smaller than the family's primary income. This family is losing a substantial portion of its overall income, and the family has less than three months' savings available. As you will see, however, with some creative financial management and cost cutting, this family can survive at least a year without this second income, surely enough time for the second wage earner to find another job. The worksheet that follows shows this family's monthly budget.

One additional note: The tax figures are approximates for a two-income family earning $75,000 and living in Ohio. Your own state and local taxes may vary and you can get accurate tax information from your most recent pay stub or by calling your former employer's payroll office. In addition, your real estate tax may vary substantially from this example.

MONTHLY BUDGET: TWO-INCOME FAMILY

Expenses

Taxes	$1625	Federal, FICA, State, Local
Mortgage	850	House payment only
House Tax/Insurance	210	Real estate taxes, house insurance
Retirement/401K	150	Part going to 401K
Life Insurance	30	Term insurance
Health Insurance	30	Employee contribution
Food	500	All items bought at grocery store

Lunch at Office	100	Extra spent on lunch
Eating Out	150	Two-income families tend to eat out more
Utilities	160	Gas, electric, water, phone, trash
Car Payment	400	Based on two cars
Car Insurance	90	Prorated, based on semiannual payments
Transportation	250	Gas, parking, based on one person having to pay for parking
Day Care	600	Professional day care for two children
Housecleaning	125	Cleaning twice per month
Clothes/Dry Cleaning	300	New purchases and dry cleaning
Donations	100	Combined charitable donations
Christmas/Vacation, etc.	100	Combined savings for Christmas, vacations, other general items
Gifts/Entertainment	200	Money spent on gifts, theater, movies, etc.
College Loan	100	Payments on one college loan
Miscellaneous	180	Anything else you can't account for
TOTAL MONTHLY	$6250	

Income

	Month	**Year**
Income #1 (lost due to layoff)	*$3000	$36,000
Income #2	$3250	$39,000
TOTAL	$6250	$75,000

*This income is lost due to a layoff, but individual receives $1000/month in unemployment compensation for the first 26 weeks of unemployment. In addition, this individual received a lump-sum severance payment of $1000.

TOTAL SAVINGS: $12,500, which includes the $1500 severance payment. Note, however, that this also includes $5000 in a 401K account that the family cannot touch without paying a penalty.

You can see from this worksheet that this family currently needs to find $2000 per month in order to balance their family budget. Before the family lost income #1, expenses and income roughly balanced at $6250 per month. Now, however, one income has been reduced from $3000 per month to approximately $1000 per month that is received as unemployment compensation.

This family's first decision was to put the $1500 received as severance pay into savings, increasing total savings to $12,500. As mentioned in Chapter 6, you should always try to hold on to any cash as long as possible and put off paying any debts as long as you can.

In order to survive for a year without this second income, this family has to cut $2000 out of its budget for the first six months, and $3000 for the second six months. (Remember that unemployment compensation generally only lasts for six months. Although it can be extended in some cases, you shouldn't count on it at this point.)

Automatic Budget Cuts

The first area to cut comes automatically: Because the family has lost one income, its monthly withholdings for federal, state, FICA, and local taxes immediately drop. Total witholding for these taxes becomes approximately $1100 when the second income is lost. (Remember that unemployment compensation *is* taxable.) Even though the family pays some taxes on unemployment compensation already, the family is able to cut $525 from its budget.

Nonessentials Next

Next, you should look at obvious areas in which you can save. This family is currently spending $600 per month on day care. As mentioned in Chapter 6, the family can realize an immediate savings by keeping both children at home. Remember that this may cause some hardship on whichever of you is currently out of work and looking for a job. You will need to have family members and friends on call who can baby-sit during interviews. However, because it involves such a large amount and such an obvious way to save money, it should be this family's next budget cut.

Similarly, having someone come in to do your housecleaning is a luxury you cannot afford while you are unemployed. For this family, canceling the housecleaning service saves $125 per month.

This family's transportation costs are $250 per month. By being out of work, the unemployed individual automatically spends less on gas, in this case a savings of $30 per month. The second individual currently pays $150 per month in parking, a figure that can be reduced by half if this person carpools or takes public transportation. Overall, this family can cut at least $100 out of its transportation budget monthly while one member of the family is unemployed.

The next category of savings comes from such "nice to have"

items as entertainment, gifts, dinner out, lunch out at the office, and other nonessential items. This group offers ample possibility for additional budget savings for this family. The before and after columns below show how this family can save in these areas:

	Before	After
Donations	$100	$50
Christmas/Vacation Savings	$100	$0
Gifts/Entertainment	$200	$50
Clothes/Dry Cleaning	$300	$150
Eating Out	$150	$50
Lunch at Office	$100	$50
Total	$950	$350

Cutting these items from the budget will be painful: You cannot go out to dinner unless it's for fast food. Entertainment will be reduced to a rented videotape once a week. The family member still working will have to carry his or her lunch to work every day. Painful as they may seem, however, these cuts can have an immediate impact on your family budget, freeing you from money anxieties that may make it difficult for you to concentrate on finding a new job right now.

After the Nonessentials

If you've been keeping track, this family still needs to cut $50 from its monthly budget for the first six months. If you have cut out all the nonessentials and still come up short on your monthly budget, you have two options to consider: You can begin taking money out of savings, or you can negotiate with your creditors for reduced payments on money you owe.

As mentioned in Chapter 6, you should try to hang on to savings as long as possible. Always keep as much cash on hand as you possibly can in order to ensure that you have something in reserve in case of emergencies.

At this point, it might be wise to talk to the companies to which you currently owe money. Call your mortgage lender and arrange to meet with them about paying interest only on your loan for a few months. Send a letter to the bank that holds your car loan and ask to work out a reduced payment plan for a few months. Remember, creditors want to avoid legal maneuverings as much as you do. This family's $50 shortfall after removing all nonessentials from the budget can come from negotiations with lenders to which they owe money.

Don't Touch Those Savings

Don't forget, however, that this family will likely lose its $1000 per month unemployment compensation after the first six months. Although many people find employment within six months of losing a job, some do not. Your initial plan should keep your family safe for up to a year, ample time to find another job.

After six months, this family will likely have to begin taking money out of savings. You can see that if the unemployed wage earner is out of work for an entire year, this family will deplete nearly all of its savings, with the exception of its 401K savings. If you get to the point at which you have exhausted all other options and are taking money out of savings, remember to use first those savings that do not have some sort of penalty for withdrawal of funds. Don't touch 401K or IRA funds if you can possibly help it.

It's Not as Hard as It Looks

Remember, there are many creative ways for your family to save money while you are out of work. Setting up a comprehensive budget and getting the whole family involved will immediately reduce your money anxieties and allow you to concentrate on finding a new job.

If you don't have any savings and have more debt than the family illustrated here, you may have to be more creative in how you cut items from your budget. Look at the ideas presented in Chapter 6 and use them to negotiate payment plans with lenders that will allow you to stay afloat while you are unemployed.

The two-income family budget illustrated earlier in this chapter now looks like this:

MONTHLY BUDGET: TWO-INCOME FAMILY
(After Cuts)

Expenses

Taxes	$1100	Federal, FICA, State, Local
Mortgage	800	Negotiated reduced payment
House Tax/Insurance	210	Real estate taxes, house insurance
Retirement/401K	150	Part going to 401K
Life Insurance	30	Term insurance
Health Insurance	30	Employee contribution
Food	500	All items bought at grocery store
Lunch at Office	50	Carry lunch to work when possible
Eating Out	50	Only fast food once or twice
Utilities	160	Gas, electric, water, phone, trash
Car Payment	400	Based on two cars

Car Insurance	90	Prorated, based on semiannual payments
Transportation	150	Employed family member carpools, takes bus
Day Care	0	Children stay home, friends help out
Housecleaning	0	Family cleans house together
Clothes/Dry Cleaning	150	New clothes only when absolutely necessary, dry cleaning only when absolutely necessary
Donations	50	Combined charitable donations
Christmas/Vacation, etc.	0	Hold off on these savings for now
Gifts/Entertainment	50	Cut way back on entertainment
College Loan	100	Payments on one college loan
Miscellaneous	180	Anything else you can't account for
TOTAL MONTHLY	$4250	

Income

	Month
Income #1 (first six months)	$1000
Income #2	$3250
TOTAL	$4250

Second six months: Take $1000 per month out of savings. Family will still have $6500 in savings at the end of the year.

THE SINGLE-EARNER WORKSHEET

If you are single and have no other source of income, you can still survive for months—even a year—without your income. You need to follow the same steps as a two-income family, making sure that you hold on to any savings you have as long as possible. You should outline your total budget and determine the essential and nonessential items on which you currently spend your salary.

Because you have only one income, you are more likely to need some sort of assistance to help you through an extended period of unemployment. Before you consider a loan, though, make sure you have an accurate picture of your current expenses. The worksheet that follows shows an example of a budget for a single person.

Remember that taxes in this example are approximates for a single person earning $36,000 and living in Ohio. Your own state and local taxes may vary, and you can get accurate tax information from your most recent pay stub or by calling your former employer's payroll office.

MONTHLY BUDGET: SINGLE INCOME

Expenses

Taxes	$1000	Federal, FICA, State, Local
Rent	500	Rent payment (includes heat)
Retirement/401K	50	Part going to 401K
Life Insurance	15	Term insurance
Health Insurance	25	Employee contribution
Food	200	All items bought at grocery store

Lunch at Office	100	Extra spent on lunch
Eating Out	150	With dates, etc.
Utilities	50	Electric, water, phone
Credit Card Payments	50	Monthly balance on one card
Car Payment	200	One car loan
Car Insurance	50	Prorated, based on semiannual payments
Transportation	100	Gas, etc.
Clothes/Dry Cleaning	225	New purchases and dry cleaning
Donations	50	Combined charitable donations
Gifts/Entertainment	100	Money spent on gifts, theater, movies, etc.
College Loan	100	Payments on one college loan
Miscellaneous	35	Anything else you can't account for
TOTAL	$3000	

Income

	Month	Year
Income (lost due to layoff)	$3000	$36,000

*This income is lost due to a layoff, but individual receives $780/month in unemployment compensation. In addition, this individual received $4000 in severance pay.

TOTAL SAVINGS: $7000, which includes the $4000 severance payment. Note, however, that this also includes $2000 in a 401K account that cannot be withdrawn without a penalty.

At the outset, this individual's monthly income drops from $3000 per month to $780 per month, making the budgeting process a significant challenge. However, as Chapter 6 illustrated, there are many creative ways to survive for several months without an income.

If you are a single person with one source of income, your first budgeting step should be to put any severance pay you receive into savings. Hold on to any cash you have for as long as possible. Next, you should be prepared to have to borrow money. As soon as you find yourself out of a job, determine what sources you have for loans.

If you own a house, you should find out about home equity loans as soon as possible. If, as in this example, you do not own a home, you will have to look at other options. As soon as you find out you are out of work, you can call the customer service numbers for any credit cards you may own and ask to have your limit increased. If you have been a good customer all along, you should have little problem increasing your limits. Remember, you want to avoid any debt possible while you are out of work, but a higher credit card balance is better than the alternative of being unable to afford basic necessities.

Automatic Budget Cuts

As with the two-income example, the first area to cut comes automatically: monthly withholdings for federal, state, FICA, and local taxes immediately drop. Total withholding for these taxes becomes essentially zero for a single earner out of work. Already, this single earner can cut $1000 from the budget.

Nonessentials Next

Cut nonessential items first. In this example, the single wage earner should cut the following items:

	Before	**After**
Retirement/401K	$ 50	$ 0
Lunch at Office	100	0
Eating Out	150	0
Transportation	100	50
Clothes/Dry Cleaning	225	25
Donations	50	0
Gifts/Entertainment	100	10
TOTAL	$775	$85

Cutting nonessential items immediately cuts $690 from the budget. These cuts may seem drastic: If you lose your only source of income, you won't be able to eat out or buy clothes until you find another job. Remember, these items are not essential to your financial survival.

After the Nonessentials

After deducting taxes and nonessential items, this single earner still needs $545 per month in addition to his or her unemployment compensation. As in this example, your two largest payments (not including taxes and nonessentials) are probably your car payment and monthly rent payments. These are two payments you should negotiate on immediately. Remember, if you have a good payment history and you explain your situation immediately, you will have a better chance of temporarily reducing your payments.

Realistically, you may be able to reduce your rent payment by $100 to $200 per month. If you negotiate with the bank that holds your car loan, you may be able to reduce it by half or more, depending on the size of the loan. Because most landlords and lenders want to avoid the difficulties and costs associated with eviction or repossession, your good-faith negotiations should be met with a receptive attitude.

If you have any other debts, write creditors a letter explaining your situation and offer to make good-faith payments. In this example, a good-faith payment of $5 per month reduces this single earner's credit card payment by $45 per month. The same holds true for college loans you may still owe. A monthly good-faith payment of $10 may be enough to keep you in good standing with the bank, assuming that you write to explain your situation as soon as you find yourself out of work.

Negotiate with utility companies to reduce your payments if possible. Some utility companies have special programs for un-employed people. Take advantage of any available programs.

In a best-case scenario, then, this single-wage earner should be able to cut his or her budget to a more manageable one, as shown on this page.

MONTHLY BUDGET: SINGLE INCOME

Expenses

Taxes	$ 0	Federal, FICA, State, Local
Rent	350	Rent payment (negotiated with landlord)
Retirement/401K	0	Do without for now
Life Insurance	15	Term insurance
Health Insurance	25	Employee contribution (can't afford to do without)
Food	125	With careful budgeting
Lunch at Office	0	None required now
Eating Out	0	Do without for now
Utilities	15	Negotiated with utility companies

Credit Card Payments	5	Negotiated good-faith payment
Car Payment	100	Negotiated reduction
Car Insurance	50	Prorated, based on semiannual payments
Transportation	50	Gas, etc.
Clothes/Dry Cleaning	25	Do without any new clothes
Donations	0	Stop donations temporarily
Gifts/Entertainment	10	Rent videos
College Loan	10	Good-faith payment negotiated with bank
Miscellaneous	0	Cut back on miscellaneous expenses —account for *everything*
TOTAL	$780	

Income

	Month
Income	$780

With very tight budgeting, it is possible for this person to reduce his or her expenses to $780 per month. After the first six months, however, his or her unemployment compensation will run out and the entire $780 per month will have to come from savings. If this person is unemployed for an entire year, he or she will deplete nearly all available savings, with the exception of 401K savings.

As you can see, the key to both of these budget plans is having some money in savings at the outset. If you have little or no savings, you will likely have to borrow money to survive beyond the end of your unemployment benefit period.

STAYING IN CONTROL

Once you have developed an effective budget, make sure you stay in control of all your financial obligations. Be sure to communicate your financial situation to every member in the family, so that everyone understands his or her contribution to the family's financial survival. Pinching pennies can be trying at times, but if you watch your budget closely, you will be able to maintain a sense of security that will guide you and your family through this difficult time.

8 | Looking for a Job

One unemployed woman wasn't sure how much to tell prospective employers about her situation. She remembers that, at the beginning, "When I went on interviews early on, I just told them I was still with the company. I didn't feel this was a problem, because I was still on the payroll under the terms of my severance agreement. But after a number of months, I wasn't sure *what* to tell them. I was afraid that if I said I was laid off, they'd always wonder, 'Why her and not someone else?' "

Looking for a new job presents a complex set of challenges by itself. If you are out of a job and looking for a new one, the challenges take on a different form: How much time will it take to find a new job? What *do* you tell prospective employers about your employment situation? What if they want to talk to your (now former) manager? As you read this chapter, you'll realize that the best advice for someone who is employed and looking for a job is also the best advice for someone who is out of work and job hunting.

START RIGHT AWAY

When you're out of a job, people will tell you a lot of things to make you feel better. One of the most common pieces of advice you'll hear is, "Being laid off is probably the best thing that could happen to you. You have your severance pay—why don't you just take some time off?" Losing your job is a traumatic experience that may make you feel you'd just like to take some time off and relax before starting your job search.

The problem is, a day or two can stretch to a week, which can become a month, and before you know it, you've been on two interviews and your severance pay runs out next week. You need to start right away because you have to get "back up on the horse," because you need to work your network while it's still fresh, but mostly because finding a job takes time.

How Long Will This Take?

Judging how long your job search will take is an inexact science. Everyone will tell you horror stories of their brother-in-law who was still looking two years later. For the record, during an average year in the 1980s, about 40 percent of unemployed people found a new job within 5 weeks of losing a job. An additional 30 percent found jobs during a period of 5 to 14 weeks after they lost their previous jobs. This means that, in an average year, about 70 percent of unemployed people find jobs within 15 weeks of being fired or laid off.

Statistics can, however, lull you into a false sense of security. When you factor in the millions of minimum-wage workers who can find another position almost immediately, you can see that the statistics can be skewed. Drake Beam Morin, a New York outplacement firm, estimates that it can take experienced professionals five to six months to find new positions. Generally, the higher your income or more specialized your interests, the longer it will take you to find a new job.

Other factors, such as the health of the economy, the demand for your skills in the job market, your willingness to relocate, and your education and experience can have an impact on the length of your search.

Regardless of your situation, then, you should begin your search immediately. Almost everyone can tell you of someone they know who was looking for a year or more before finding another position. As you learned in Chapter 6, with some judicious financial juggling you should easily be able to tough it out for at least nine months to a year. The sooner you start your job search, though, the more likely you will be to find a new job within a significantly shorter time frame.

What Will It Cost?

You will have a number of expenses as you proceed with your job search. Because you need to conserve financial resources right now, you need to be judicious about what you spend on your job search. A number of potential costs include:

> *Resumé preparation.* You'll learn more about resumé preparation later in this chapter. Resumé services can help you prepare a resumé, but they can charge several hundred dollars for their service. A cheaper alternative is to write your own, using some of the guidelines in this chapter and the advice of other experts on the subject. A good book on resumé preparation can save you many times its cost in resumé preparation fees. You can still expect to pay for stationery, envelopes, and printing costs, depending on how you have your resumé printed. In general, a neat typing job is all that is necessary; typesetting or laser printing adds to your costs without adding any appreciable value.

Recruiters. You should never pay a recruiter a fee for finding you a job. In general, recruiters are paid by the company that has the job opening. More information on recruiters is included in this chapter.

You may also have to buy an occasional lunch for key people in your network of contacts or pay for dry cleaning for your interview suits. In general, you can keep costs down by doing as much as you can (resumé preparation, typing, and other tasks) on your own. Books can substitute as inexpensive "experts," giving you a wealth of information for very little cost.

You should definitely keep track of everything you spend on your job search because your expenses may be tax-deductible. According to Robert McCarthy, president of a financial advisory firm in Massachussetts, "The more you spend on your job search, the more likely it is that some of your expenses will be deductible." In fact, if you itemize your taxes, and if your job-search expenses exceed 2 percent of your adjusted gross income, you can take a deduction for those expenses.

Most of the expenses you incur when looking for a job fall into this tax-deductible category. You should keep track of everything, including:

- mileage to and from meetings with prospective employers or people in your job-search network, as well as tolls and parking expenses

- any other travel expenses, especially if you are looking for a job out of town

- meal expenses that are involved

- office supplies, stationery, and postage

- job-search services, resumé services, and job-search books

You should be aware that job-search-related deductions can only be deducted if you are looking for a new position in your present field. In other words, an industrial engineer looking for another engineering position may be able to deduct her expenses while an accountant looking for a job as a teacher would not.

You may want to contact the IRS to determine if your expenses are deductible. In addition, you must keep accurate and complete records to protect yourself in the event you are audited by the IRS. Keep a diary or ledger detailing your job-search activities (whom you met or had lunch with, how many miles you traveled, and so forth) and keep *every* receipt. If you are unsure about the laws, you should contact a tax professional or the IRS.

WHAT DO YOU WANT TO DO?

If you've been a research director for a consumer products firm for the past 10 years, your first instinct will be to put together a resumé and send it to other consumer products firms. The desire to find employment quickly can force you to make decisions without really assessing what it is you want to do. Being suddenly unemployed can be an unnerving experience, but it can also provide you with an opportunity to reassess yourself, your career to date, and your true interests.

"The goal," according to career development specialist Dr. Daniel H. Averbeck, "should be to change your focus from merely finding another job to finding work that truly satisfies you." Most people never stop to assess if their occupations truly fit them. Being laid off can give you an opportunity to stop and consider what you'd really like to do. "You can look at being laid off as an *opportunity*, rather than as the most horrible thing to ever happen to you," Dr. Averbeck contends. This kind of self-assessment takes time, but right now you can afford a day or two to determine what is important to you before you continue your career.

As mentioned in the introduction to this book, some of the

most successful people have been fired at one time in their lives. Steven Jobs was fired from Apple Computer, one of the world's most successful computer companies and a company he founded. Instead of viewing this situation as a personal failure, Jobs used the opportunity to focus his thinking and forge ahead with new ideas and plans. Within two years he founded NeXT, Inc., a computer company that eventually found backing from such industry giants as IBM.

What Is Important to You?

You may have been too busy climbing the corporate ladder to ever stop and ask yourself important career questions. Now that the ladder has been, in effect, pulled out from under you, you have the chance to ask those questions. Start by assessing what is really important to you. Make a list of 20 criteria you can use to assess future career goals. Write them down as you think of them, in no particular order. Your list may have some of the following items:

- Prestige

- Money

- More time with family

- Stay in this area

- Travel less (or travel more)

- More creative work

- Less administrative detail

- Learn new technologies

- Smaller (or larger) company

When you complete the list, put the items in order of importance, starting with the most important items first. Be brutally honest with yourself as you develop your list. Don't say money isn't important if you're unwilling to live without the sports car.

If you are married, ask your spouse to make a similar list and put it in order also. You may find that his or her priorities are very different from yours. Money may be less important to him than you thought. She may really wish that you'd follow some of those entrepreneurial dreams you've always had. The point of this exercise is to look at what matters to you, and to focus your job search on jobs that will allow you to do more of what you want to do.

You may find that you got into sales because you wanted to make more money, but that when you really think about it, you'd rather be home more often. Or, you may realize that the huge corporate structure you thought made you feel secure was actually stifling your abilities. A smaller company may offer you challenges you may never have considered.

The result of this exercise may be a decision to make minor changes in your career path. On the other hand, you may make major changes you never thought you'd make: You may change careers altogether, go back to school, or start your own business.

Even if financial concerns require you to take a less attractive position right away, don't abandon the process. You can still take steps to make happen what you'd like to have happen. Save to start the company or go to night school while you work. "The point is," Dr. Averbeck advises, "if you take a job that isn't exactly what you want to do, be aware of why you are taking it, and keep working toward something that really does fit."

DEFINING YOUR JOB SEARCH

Once you've defined what you want to do, you need to objectively review your qualifications. If you've decided to make a drastic career change, you may need to take it one step at a time: Look for a job you're qualified for first, then work towards the job you'd ultimately like to do.

Before you send a single resumé, you need to set some realistic goals. Setting realistic goals is important, especially if you have been out of the job market for a number of years. You may be completely unaware of your own marketability, making it even more important to get an objective opinion on your goals. As you define the type of position you seek right now, you should try to be as specific as possible. Think about all aspects of the job you are looking for, including:

> *Management level.* When you begin your search, if you are targeting a position above your current level of experience, your job search can be significantly extended. Even if you believe you should have been promoted by your former employer but never were, you should not go looking for a position at a higher management level than your current experience supports.

> *Job function.* Your self-assessment should have provided you with ideas on the job function you'd like to perform. As you set your goals, though, you should outline several job functions you have the experience to perform, even if they are not your first choice for a new position. For example, if you have most recently been involved in marketing but have a degree and experience in accounting, both types of job functions can offer you immediate opportunities.

> *Industry.* As with your job function, you may need to look at more than one target industry. To fulfill your immediate financial needs, you may need to look outside of the industry that would be your first choice.

Your Target Companies

Once you've defined your job-search criteria, you need to determine what companies or organizations in what geographic locations need the skills and experience you can provide. Again, outplacement services can help you create a list of target companies. If you don't have access to an outplacement service or career guidance counselor, your local library's government and business section can help. You can get listings of companies by industry code, and the library may maintain a card file or directory of information on local companies.

Once you have defined the job you are looking for and created a list of target companies, you can begin your job search. The rest of this chapter discusses job-search tactics you can use, and how to deal with some of the questions and concerns that arise for an unemployed person currently looking for a job.

RESUMÉS

No matter what techniques you use to look for a job, the most important tool you can use is an effective resumé. Richard Beatty, a specialist in the area of human resources and the author of *The Resumé Kit*, lists eight important characteristics of a good resumé:

- neat
- well-organized
- easily and quickly read
- organized so that key information is highly visible
- appropriate in length (not too long or too short)

- includes brief yet complete job descriptions

- depicts key accomplishments

- provides a complete accounting of key areas of interest to a prospective employer

If you haven't been in the job market for a number of years, you may not have updated your resumé for quite some time. Creating an effective resumé can be a complex process that can be complicated by the fact that you are currently out of work. How do you reflect your current job situation on your resumé? Should your first entry state "19XX to *Present*"? Should you even use a chronological format at all?

As you develop your resumé, you need to concentrate more on highlighting your accomplishments and less on the fact that you are currently out of work. The format of your resumé can help you do this. Most experts on resumés agree that the most effective resumé format is the chronological format, one in which your education and experience are listed in chronological order, with your most recent position listed first. An example of a chronological resumé follows.

Krystina P. Smith
818 Endline Road
Cincinnati, Ohio 45001
Phone: (513)808-0808

OBJECTIVE: Director of software product marketing for a software company.

EDUCATION: M.B.A., Xavier University, 1982
Major: Marketing, GPA: 3.5/4.0

B.S., Ohio State University, 1974
Major: Computer Science, GPA: 3.7/4.0

EMPLOYMENT:

1980–1990   *Technical Information Systems, Inc.*

Director, Software Product Marketing
(1988–1990)
Reported directly to Vice President,
Market Development with full marketing
responsibility for MS-DOS database and
fourth-generation language products.
Directed the activities of two product
marketing managers, one market
research manager, twelve marketing
specialists, and eight market research
specialists. Increased overall customer
satisfaction ratings by more than 30
percent in three years. Responsible for
strategic planning, including pricing,
market positioning, and analysis of
customer satisfaction data.

Product Marketing Manager (1984–1988)
Reported to Director, Software Product
Marketing. Responsible for market
research and development of a new
fourth-generation language product for
software developers. Product captured
20 percent market share within two
years of initial product release.
Received *Dataview* magazine product
quality award in 1986. Managed the
activities of four marketing specialists

Marketing Specialist (1982–1984)
Responsible for creating customer

surveys and for analyzing customer survey data. Created and maintained customer contact database to ensure attainment of quality assurance goals. Participated in business plan development for new fourth-generation language product.

Programmer/Analyst (1980–1982)
Reported directly to manager, Product Development. Managed two programmers in the advanced technology research group. Researched artificial intelligence tools to determine applicability to company's current product set. Designed prototype natural language interface to microcomputer-based database.

1974–1980   *Info Telemarketing Corp.*

Programmer/Analyst 1976–1980
Designed and programmed databases to track customer responses to market research questionnaires. Developed custom reports to support market research projects for several major customers. Managed two programmers and programmer assistant.

Computer Programmer 1974–1976
Programmed in C and fourth-generation languages. Responsible for maintaining market research databases. Designed report formats to project specifications.

PROFESSIONAL
ACTIVITIES: Member, American Marketing
Association

PERSONAL: Age 39
Married, two children
U.S. Citizen
Excellent health

References furnished upon request.

As you look at the resumé, you'll notice that one drawback of a chronological resumé is that it highlights the dates of your employment. In other words, if you have been out of work for some time, it will be immediately obvious. There are several things you can do to downplay the significance of employment dates without drawing attention to them.

First, if you have recently lost your job and are still receiving severance pay, technically, you can say you are still employed by the company. In that case, the first entry on your resumé should read "19XX to Present." You will need to be careful about this approach if there is any possibility that a prospective employer is aware of your employment situation. For example, if your former employer closed a regional office, leaving you out of a job, it will be common knowledge in the community.

If you have been out of work for a longer period of time (well beyond the end of your severance agreement) or if you don't feel you can honestly state that you are currently employed by your previous employer, you need to modify your resumé to reflect that fact without giving it undue attention.

A few simple modifications can draw less attention to the dates on your resumé while still showing a reasonable chronological progression in your employment history. The resumé format that follows shows one example of how to do this.

Krystina P. Smith
818 Endline Road
Cincinnati, Ohio 45001
Phone: (513)808-0808

OBJECTIVE: Director of software product marketing for a software company.

EDUCATION: M.B.A., Xavier University, 1982
Major: Marketing, GPA: 3.5/4.0

B.S., Ohio State University, 1974
Major: Computer Science, GPA: 3.7/4.0

EMPLOYMENT: *Technical Information Systems, Inc.*

Director, Software Product Marketing
Promoted in 1988 to Director, reporting directly to Vice President, Market Development with full marketing responsibility for MS-DOS database and fourth-generation language products. Responsible for the activities of two product marketing managers, one market research manager, twelve marketing specialists, and eight market research specialists. Increased overall customer satisfaction ratings by more than 30 percent in three years. Responsible for strategic planning, including pricing, market positioning, and analysis of customer satisfaction data.

Product Marketing Manager
Due to outstanding achievement,
promoted in 1984 to Manager. Reported
to Director, Software Product Marketing.
Responsible for market research and
development of a new fourth-generation
language product for software
developers. Product captured 20 percent
market share within two years of initial
product release. Received *Dataview*
magazine product quality award in
1986. Managed the activities of four
marketing specialists.

Marketing Specialist
Upon completing M.B.A in 1982,
transferred to Marketing. Responsible
for creating customer surveys and for
analyzing customer survey data.
Created and maintained customer
contact database to ensure attainment
of quality assurance goals. Participated
in business plan development for new
fourth-generation language product.

Programmer/Analyst
Joined company in product development
in 1980. Reported directly to manager,
Product Development. Managed two
programmers in the advanced
technology research group. Researched
artificial intelligence tools to determine
applicability to company's current
product set. Designed prototype natural
language interface to microcomputer-
based database.

Info Telemarketing Corp.

Programmer/Analyst
Promoted in 1976 to Programmer/
Analyst. Designed and programmed
databases to track customer responses
to market research questionnaires.
Developed custom reports to support
market research projects for several
major customers. Managed two
programmers and a programmer
assistant.

Computer Programmer
Joined company in 1974. Programmed in
C and fourth-generation languages.
Responsible for maintaining market
research databases. Designed report
formats to project specifications.

PROFESSIONAL
ACTIVITIES: Member, American Marketing
Association

PERSONAL: Age 39
Married, two children
U.S. Citizen
Excellent health

References furnished upon request.

As you can see, this second format is still clear and easy to
read. However, it does not specifically state that you are no longer
with your last employer. This format does a better job of calling
attention to your abilities without drawing attention to the fact

that you are currently unemployed. By using such phrases as "responsible for" instead of "directed the activities of," you avoid using the past tense and reduce the chance that a prospective employer will question whether you are still employed.

As you complete your resumé, remember that you need to be sure that it represents you well, without telling a prospective employer more than he or she needs to know. You have a much better chance of explaining your situation face to face than in a resumé or cover letter. Because of this, you need to be sure that your resumé doesn't call attention to your current employment status, but it also doesn't appear to be hiding anything.

Once you complete your resumé, it's a good idea to have it reviewed by someone who can give you objective criticism you can use to improve your resumé. Find someone with a background in human resources (perhaps through your former employer, especially if they offered to help in your search), and have that person objectively review your resumé. Someone who screens resumés on a daily basis will be able to spot obvious errors. Make sure your reviewer has experience reading or preparing resumés.

If you can't find an expert who can review your resumé, compare it to sample resumés in any one of a number of good books available on the subject of resumé writing. Some of the better ones available are listed at the end of this chapter.

A Good Cover Letter

Like a resumé, a cover letter is often your first contact with a prospective employer. As with your resumé, your cover letter should mention as little as possible about your current employment situation. You will have more success in explaining your situation in person than if you let a resumé or cover letter do it for you.

For that reason, your cover letter should not discuss the fact that you are currently unemployed, nor should it mention the reasons behind your previous employer's decision to let you go. Even if your layoff was motivated by significant financial problems, you should avoid mention of it in your cover letter. Again, you need to explain the situation in person to a prospective employer to ensure that there are no misunderstandings. For more ideas on how to do this, see "Preparing for the Interview" later in this chapter.

Your cover letter needs to attract your potential employer's attention and sell your abilities. It must be neat, well written, easy to read, and, above all, free from any grammatical or typographical errors. In *The Perfect Cover Letter*, Michael Beatty suggests that a good cover letter has:

- an introductory paragraph that is interest-generating and states or implies employment interest

- a value-selling paragraph that demonstrates the value you add to the prospective company and highlights your key strengths and abilities

- a background summary paragraph that briefly summarizes your relevant education and experience

- a statement that compels or ensures follow-up action

- a statement of appreciation

The following cover letter includes these important points.

1404 Jacquard Street
Cleveland, OH 44131
September 5, 1992

Mr. Frank Williams
Director of Corporate Accounting

Allied Paper Corp.
1800 Technecenter Drive
Cleveland, OH 44102

Dear Mr. Williams:

The July 15 issue of *Paper Industry* magazine lists Allied Paper Corp. as one of the best-run companies in the industry. The article noted the company's success in financial planning and management. Because your organization plays a critical part in that success, I am very interested in working for you.

My six years of public accounting experience together with my experience on accounts in your industry can add significant value to your staff. My attention to details has helped many of my clients identify and reduce unnecessary expenses.

I am a certified public accountant with a B.S. in accounting. In the coming spring, I will receive my M.B.A. in accounting.

I would appreciate the opportunity to discuss how my qualifications can add to your staff's recognized achievements. I will call you on September 12 to determine your interest and, if appropriate, to arrange a personal meeting.

I look forward to meeting with you.

Sincerely,

Myrle M. Sammonds

Enclosure

As with your resumé, any advice you can get from a competent reviewer can help you polish your cover letter. In addition, several of the books listed at the end of this chapter can give you more ideas on how to write cover letters that effectively present your abilities.

SOURCES OF JOB LEADS

You've determined the companies that are likely to need your skills, and you've developed a resumé and had it reviewed by an expert. You've devised an enticing and professional cover letter that you're sure will get you noticed. How do you get your resumé and, more importantly, *yourself* in front of the right people? How do you get your foot in the door?

There are a number of methods you can use to get access to potential employers. Most job-search experts agree that an effective job-search campaign should involve as many methods as possible. For example, many people out of work scan the newspaper classified section every Sunday, looking for appropriate positions and responding to them. You may be surprised to learn that only 10 to 14 percent of all open positions are filled through advertising. Responding to ads in the newspaper should be just one of the many tactics you use to find a new job. The rest of this chapter describes some of the more effective methods you can use.

USING YOUR NETWORK

You know it's true: Most jobs are not advertised in newspapers. In fact, employment experts believe nearly two-thirds of all jobs are filled through personal contact. Richard Beatty, author of *The Complete Job Search Book*, believes networking is "the one employment strategy that seems to have the unanimous support of both seasoned employment and outplacement professionals alike. The reason for this is simple: It works!"

Interestingly, the only drawback to networking as an effective job-search method is that it takes a great deal of time to execute effectively. This is the one area in which you have a distinct advantage over someone who is already employed and looking for a job: You have plenty of time. If you think about it, this advantage is significant: The single most important method for finding a job is also the one you are currently best suited to employ.

The success of networking is based on the simple principle that someone working for a particular company is likely to hear about new positions opening within that company. The more employed people you have in your network, the more job leads your network will create for you.

Every person you know or come in contact with just may have a job lead for you. When you are unemployed, you'll be amazed at how many of these people will go out of their way to help you. To coordinate your networking efforts, first make a list of everyone you know who could have contacts that would help you. This list should be as broad as possible: Your dentist isn't a chemical engineer, but some of his patients might be. Your list should be as comprehensive as possible. Here are some ideas:

Your former boss	Your minister
Previous bosses	Insurance agent
Previous co-workers	Your car pool
College friends	Family dentist
Government contacts	Family doctor
Your softball team	Neighbors
Relatives	Military contacts
Your accountant	Former clients
Your attorney	Other friends

As you start to make your list, you'll begin to realize that the number of contacts you have is virtually endless. Any one of them may know of a job you should apply for or may be aware of someone who can lead you to an opening. If you use these contacts wisely, instead of being one of thousands of responses to an advertisement, you can become a recognized and recommended candidate.

If you haven't kept in touch with some of these people for quite some time, you may feel somewhat uneasy about calling them for help at this time. You should remember that most people genuinely enjoy helping others, as long as you are reasonable in your request. If you ask a neighbor to arrange a meeting for you with the president of his company, you may be asking too much. However, if you ask him to introduce you to colleagues he thinks you should be talking to, he'll probably be happy to help.

Believe it or not, one of the most immediate benefits of being unemployed is that many people will go out of their way to try to help you. In the last couple of decades, job uncertainty has become a fact of life in most industries. People will be sympathetic towards your situation out of concern for you but also because they'll realize it could happen to them someday—then they'll be calling you.

Once you've listed the people in your network, you need to begin contacting them. Your goals in contacting these people should be:

- to let them know you are looking for a job and ask them for their support

- to briefly describe your background

- to ask them if they are aware of specific positions you should apply for

- to expand your network by asking them for names of other people you should be contacting

- to ask if you can use their names or if they would personally introduce you to someone they think you should be talking to

Depending on how well you know the person, you may want to be very candid about your current employment situation. If the person is someone you think may have a current opening, you might want to wait until you have the interview before you discuss the details of your situation. If you're contacting a member of your church, you can explain the situation in more detail. Anyone who knows you well will empathize with your situation and be that much more willing to help you.

If you contact someone on your list and he or she has no ideas right now, don't take that name off the list. Ask if you can send a resumé and call again in a few weeks to see if he or she has learned of any potential contacts.

After you've completed calls to everyone on your list, you'll have a number of additional people to contact. These will be the names you've been given by people in your network. These people will be very important contacts for you because they will be closer to potential job openings. When calling these people, your goal should *not* be to ask them for a job. Rather, you should be looking for advice on your current search, and for more names to add to your list. Your goal in contacting these people will be to:

- introduce yourself and mention the name of the person who suggested that you call

- explain your job search and ask for his or her advice on how best to approach the target industry and companies you've identified

- ask if you can meet to discuss your search, or ask to spend a few moments on the telephone

- find out if they know of any companies looking for someone with your background and if they know of people within those companies you should be talking to

- ask for their help in getting an introduction

As you use your network, remember that your goal with everyone you talk with is *not* to ask for a job but rather to acquaint the person with your background and increase the number of contacts you have. As you continue this process, you'll eventually encounter people who are interested in talking about a specific position. People will be more open to talking with you about specific openings if you are asking for advice and contacts, rather than a job.

Other groups and organizations can help you expand your network. Some of these groups include:

Professional organizations. If you don't already belong to a professional organization, you probably cannot afford the dues for one right now. However, some of the people in your network may belong to one or more organizations. Ask if you can attend a meeting simply to make contacts.

Job fairs. A job fair can give you instant access to a number of companies at once, all of which probably have current openings. You should be aware, however, that most companies resort to job fairs to recruit hard-to-find talent, particularly in highly technical fields. Because you have the time, however, it can only help to make more contacts through job fairs.

Alumni associations and college placement programs. If you haven't kept up with your college alumni association, contact the local chapter to determine if they have placement resources. If you attended a local college or university, their placement office may be aware of companies that, in addition to recruiting college students, are also looking for people with more experience.

Recruiters and Executive Search Firms

Recruiters and executive search firms belong in the same category because they perform the same function—matching appropriate talent with appropriate openings. That is where the similarity stops, however, and you should be aware of the differences as you decide whether to use either in your search.

Executive search firms are hired *by the company* that has an open position. As their name implies, these firms generally only deal with executive talent. If you annual income is not in the executive range (starting in the $50,000 to $60,000 range), you are not a likely candidate for an executive search firm. If you do have upper-level management experience and are a likely candidate for an executive search firm, you should contact a reputable firm and arrange to meet with them. Keep in mind, though, that executive recruiters do not work for *you* but, rather, for the companies that hire them. They will only be able to help you if they happen to have an opening that happens to match your background.

If executive search firms are a finely targeted rifle working for prospective employers, recruiters are shotguns trying to make a match anywhere possible. Unfortunately, there are a few recruiting firms and recruiters that give the industry a bad name. If you want to work with a recruiter, you should be careful in choosing a reputable agency. Contact someone in your area who has been in human resources for a number of years. He or she will be able to tell you which agencies are reputable. As you choose an agency, remember:

■ Agencies rarely have an exclusive on any position. If you are working with more than one agency, be careful that they aren't both working on the same position. Potential employers will immediately have a bad impression of you if they receive your resumé from more than one agency.

■ Make sure the agency doesn't sell its client list. Again, a potential employer could end up seeing your resumé from more than one agency, leaving him or her with a bad impression.

■ Make sure the recruiter you work with promises not to send your resumé to any company unless he or she discusses it with you first. In this way, you'll avoid sending the same resumé twice.

■ Make sure any fees the agency receives are paid by the employer, not by you. The last thing you need at this time is a bill for recruiting services.

In general, if your skills are in demand in your area, a recruiter can help. If you have an unusual set of skills, recruiters may be of little value. Because each recruiter in an agency is trying to fill up to 20 positions at any one time, he or she will have little time to really understand your background and goals. If you do choose to work with a recruiter and it doesn't work well for you, tell the agency you no longer require their services. If the agency has been making bad matches for you in the attempts of finding *any* match, you may be better off without them.

PREPARING FOR INTERVIEWS

Interviews are the most important part of any job search. An interview is likely your first, and maybe your only, chance to make a positive face-to-face impression on a prospective employer. You will likely have to go through more than one interview for any position, and each one will be critical to your success.

Before you attend your first interview, you should research the interview process and learn what types of questions an interviewer is likely to ask. A number of excellent books on interview skills and questions are available. Books like *How to Turn an Interview into a Job* and *The Complete Q&A Job Interview Book* by Jeffrey Allen can help you practice critical interviewing skills.

As an unemployed job seeker, however, you have a number of additional issues to address before you meet your first interviewer. You need to be prepared to answer questions about your current situation without harming your job prospects.

Do I Tell Them I Was Laid Off?

You don't want to lie, but you're afraid the truth may harm your prospects. What do you say? There are a number of approaches to this difficult situation. They include:

> *Honesty.* If you are in an industry that is currently experiencing a great deal of turmoil (such as manufacturing, electronics, computer hardware, airline, steel manufacturers, Wall Street brokerage firms), your situation is almost the norm. In this case, honesty is the best policy. Tell your prospective employer that you were laid off because your former employer was having severe financial problems. If you plan to use this tactic, be sure to have a couple of facts on hand to support you. Mention the number of people your employer let go. Toss out a few figures about how much your previous employer lost this quarter. Your goal is not to harm your previous employer's reputation but, rather, to make it obvious that you were just one of a long line of casualties in your previous employer's losing battle with the bottom line.

You are unemployed by choice. This can be a tricky explanation. Why would a level-headed, employed individual
choose to be out of work? If your previous employer was
losing money rapidly and offering great severance pay packages, however, you may have chosen to take advantage of
the offer.

You resigned under duress. Your previous employer offered
you a stock option that never materialized, or you exceeded
your targets and didn't receive the expected bonus. When
you pressured them for it, you were pressured to leave.
There are a number of reasons you may have chosen to
leave on your own. You have to be careful, however, that
your reasons don't lead a prospective employer to wonder
if you are a difficult person to work with in general.

Before you go to an interview, practice what you will say.
Talk with others who have experience hiring people in your
situation and ask them what they expect to hear and what kinds
of statements will raise a red flag. Above all, be straightforward
yourself, and don't modify your answers if you talk with more
than one person at the same company over the course of the
interview process.

What If They Want to Talk to My Previous Employer?

Another reason to be truthful with a prospective employer is that
he or she may insist on talking with your previous manager. At
first, you may be concerned, especially if you left under less than
amicable terms. Before you go on an interview, assume your
prospective employer will want to speak with your former employer. Contact your former manager and discuss the situation
with him or her. If you were laid off due to financial problems,

he or she will probably feel relieved to be able to help you find another position.

If you were fired for any reason other than the financial health of the company, you need to know what your previous employer will say *before* he or she is given the chance. Contact your former manager and calmly discuss the situation with him or her. If you left after a heated exchange with your former manager, you may have to mend some fences. Ask him or her exactly what he plans to say. The two of you should come to an agreement on his or her responses. Your goal does not have to be to get your previous employer to make unusually wonderful comments about you but rather to ensure that he or she does not say anything damaging.

In fact, if you were terminated, you are probably protected by law from a negative reference. Your previous employer should know this. If not, you may want to point this out to him or her. Most states have antiblacklisting laws that prevent former employers from knowingly attempting to prevent former employees from finding work. Your previous employer doesn't have to give you a halo, but it's in his or her *legal* interest to refrain from condemning you.

TEMPORARY EMPLOYMENT

It's been several months and you haven't found an offer that suits you. Should you take a job you don't want while you look for another one? This complex question has many answers, all of which hinge on a number of important issues, including:

The duration of your severance agreement. If you continue to be diligent in your job search, careful about your budget, and still have more than a month's severance pay available, you can probably hold off taking a temporary job while you look for one that is a good match for you. In general, you are better off not taking a job you know you don't want if you can avoid it. Not only will this allow you to continue to work full time on your job search, you will also avoid job hopping and making commitments you cannot keep.

How long you've been looking. In Chapter 6 you learned that a family with some initial savings can probably survive for nine months to a year financially. If you have been looking for more than six months and your severance pay has run out, you may want to more carefully evaluate prospects that are not your first or second choice. Even though you want to avoid job hopping, you have every right to take a position *and* continue your search.

Availability of free-lance work. Free-lance work can provide you the best of both worlds: You can continue to look for a permanent position and still earn money to keep your family solvent. If you have experience in accounting, computer programming, technical writing, engineering, drafting, architectural design, or any other skills that may be in demand, you can use your network to look for free-lance work while you look for a permanent position.

STAY WITH IT

Finally, the best piece of advice you can take when looking for a job is to keep looking. Employed people looking for jobs have the luxury of taking their time with the process. If you are out of work and looking for a job, the prospects can seem discouraging at times. Weeks can drag on to months and your prospects can seem dim. You need to realize that your job hunt *is* your full-time job.

A job hunt is a numbers game that takes a great deal of time and effort. You certainly have the time. You need to keep up a steady effort even when you think you've exhausted all prospects. Set goals and plans on a weekly basis. If you've called your entire network once or twice, call them again. When you are unemployed and looking for a new job, time, tenacity, and perseverance are your greatest assets.

REFERENCE BOOKS

A number of excellent reference books on job searches are referenced throughout this chapter. Here is a comprehensive list of some of the best titles available:

Job Searches:

The Complete Job Search Book, Richard H. Beatty
Finding the Right Job at Midlife, Jeffrey G. Allen
The Placement Strategy Handbook, Jeffrey G. Allen

Resumés and Cover Letters:

The Resumé Kit, Richard H. Beatty
The Perfect Cover Letter, Richard H. Beatty

Interviewing Skills:

How to Turn an Interview into a Job, Jeffrey G. Allen
The Five-Minute Interview, Richard H. Beatty

9 | Honey, I Found a Job!

"I kept thinking, 'As soon as I find another job, this will all be over,' " Matt, a pharmaceutical sales representative said. "I'd start a new job, try to rebuild our savings. We'd take vacations again, and it would be as if that period of unemployment never happened. But I have a job now; I've been with this company six months. Somehow, I can't get over this feeling that I always need to be looking over my shoulder. At the end of my first month there, the sales manager called me into his office. My heart started to pound and I actually started to sweat. It turns out it was just a monthly status meeting. He does it with all the reps."

If you've ever experienced a traumatic situation, you realize that part of that trauma can stay with you long after the event is over. It's a lot like getting a telephone call in the early hours of the morning to receive the news about a death in the family. For years after the event you'll jump whenever the telephone rings at an odd hour of the night.

When you do start a new job, you need to be aware of how the experience of having lost a job can affect your attitudes towards your new employer. Some of the affects can be positive, others can have a detrimental effect on your career or family life.

You need to be aware of these affects before they happen so that you can understand your own responses and the potential impact on your career.

HOW DO YOU SPELL RELIEF?

"God, I was just so *relieved*," one woman said, recalling the day she received a job offer after having been out of work for nine months. "I tried to sound calm and professional as my future manager was telling me how impressed they were with my qualifications. He said they wanted me on board right away and wondered how soon I could start. It was all I could do to keep from laughing hysterically at this man. 'How does yesterday sound?' was all I could think. After I hung up the telephone, I sat down on the bed and sobbed uncontrollably. I couldn't believe it was finally over."

Depending on how long you have been out of work, your first job offer can seem like a cool drink of water after being lost in the desert. You don't care about much other than the fact that you *finally* have a job. You may jump at the chance and be overly willing to accept the offer, whatever the terms. At this point, you need to force yourself to think logically about the offer and what you are willing to accept. Most importantly, you should be ready and willing to negotiate.

Who's Holding the Cards?

When you receive an offer you'd like to accept, you need to think of it as just that—a first offer. If you were employed and looking for another job, you probably wouldn't accept the first offer that was given to you. You'd think about the salary, profit sharing, and benefits. You'd wonder if you should ask them to pay for parking in the company garage.

When you've been out of work, not only are you more desperate to find a job quickly, you may also be feeling uneasy about your own worth. After all, if your last employer could do without you, how much could you be worth to this new company?

What you have to realize is that negotiations are not only accepted, they are *expected* when job offers are concerned. According to Richard Beatty, author of *The Complete Job Search Book*, "it is important to realize that employers, for the most part, prefer to make offers that are at, or below, the salary range midpoint" for the position being offered. Most employers assume you will negotiate and expect such a response from a competent professional.

While there are a number of negotiation guidelines to follow, the most important one for someone who has been out of work for some time is don't panic. Don't assume that if you counter their original offer the company will rescind the offer and hire someone else. If they made the offer to you in the first place it is because you are the candidate they chose for the position. There may be others who had better credentials and cost far too much, or others who were less qualified but would cost the company less. However, because they offered *you* the job you are now in the driver's seat. As with any negotiation, you need to be reasonable, but you do need to negotiate.

Negotiate

If you are at the point of receiving an offer, you have probably already discussed salary ranges with your prospective employer. You should have a reasonable understanding of where your salary requirements fit within the range of what the company is willing to offer. If you don't know where your requirements fit with the salary range for the position, you need to do some initial investigating before you negotiate a final offer. Because you want your negotiations to appear reasonable to the company, you need to know the company's salary range for the position being offered. Beatty suggests a properly positioned request for salary range information, such as:

> Jane, what is the salary range for this position? I would prefer to avoid the situation where I might be hired near or at the range maximum. My experience has been that being compensated at this level frequently leads to future salary administration problems, making it difficult to be appropriately compensated for above average or outstanding performance. Such a situation would concern me.

Such a carefully worded request should be acceptable to the person giving you the initial offer. The more information you are able to get from the company about the offer, the more effective you can be in your negotiations.

Once you determine the salary range for the position being offered to you, you can use that information to determine your response to the company's offer. If you are able to get information about the salary range for the position, you will be better prepared to give your counter offer to the company.

As you begin your negotiations, your prospective employer will want to know what kind of offer you are looking for. You should respond with an amount that leaves the company with some room to negotiate. In addition, your amount should be slightly higher than the maximum amount you believe they are prepared to offer, realizing that they are likely to negotiate downward from your offer.

The keys to effective salary negotiations are to be reasonable and to provide a rationale to support your request. If you know that jobs for people with your qualifications are scarce or that the state of the economy has put many people with your qualifications out of work, you may need to reduce the amount you ask for. Throughout the process, don't forget that the company offering you a position has decided that, unemployed or not, you do have a definite value to them. Your salary negotiations should be reasonable, but they should also reflect the fact that you also believe you can add value to the company.

DEALING WITH LEFTOVER ANXIETY

You've received an offer, negotiated it effectively, and now you have a new job. As mentioned earlier in this chapter, the after-effects of unemployment can stay with you as you start your new job and for some time afterward. You need to understand these effects and their potential impact on your future performance.

One man recalled one of the more difficult aspects of the day he was laid off. "They called us all into a room to tell us we were out of work. Then they gave us each a cardboard printer-paper box to take our personal belongings home with us. Nobody was allowed to pack up alone, though. The company had some-one come with each of us as we cleaned out our offices, to make sure no one was taking anything that belonged to the company. They wouldn't let me take my Rolodex with me. They said that it belonged to the company. That was a year ago and it still stays with me. I now keep important business cards in a small card file that fits in my briefcase. I take it home with me every night. Just in case."

It may be hard to believe that your period of unemployment is over, much less that it won't happen again. However, leftover anxiety can prevent you from being as effective as you can be in your new position. The important thing to remember is that this stress is irrational. In fact, the real threat of future unemployment is likely to be relatively small. Just because it happened once is no guarantee that it will happen again and, as the old adage goes, you can't solve it by worrying about it.

After having been through job loss once, though, you will probably always be sensitive to changes in your new company's financial health. This heightened sensitivity can actually be a very useful defense mechanism. One of the most important lessons you can learn from having experienced job loss once is how to avoid it again in the future. Not only can you read the signs better than before (as described in Chapter 1), you are also more adept at finding a new job, should that skill ever be necessary again.

Keeping an Eye on the Future

Some experts even advise that your job search should not end just because you find another job, even if the new job is an outstanding one. In fact, some experts believe you should *never* stop looking, throughout your entire career. The ability to keep your options open at all times reduces your anxiety over having lost a job and also provides positive career-growth potential.

Paul Hirsch, author of *Pack Your Own Parachute: How to Survive Mergers, Takeovers, and Other Corporate Disasters*, believes you should always be aware of all your available career options in the event you ever again start to see the signs of impending layoffs or downsizings. Hirsch gives five strategies he believes all professionals should employ at all times during their careers:

1. Cultivate networks, maintain visibility

2. Return recruiters' calls, maintain marketability

3. Avoid overspecialization, maintain generality

4. Avoid long-term and group assignments, maintain credibility

5. Keep your bags packed, maintain mobility

You will probably never forget the experience of losing a job. You can, however, turn that leftover anxiety into a career advantage by being constantly aware of changes in your employer's stability and by being open to new career possibilities you may never have considered before you lost your job.

Recovering Your Self-Esteem

"It was one year after I started my new job, after being out of work for more than eight months," a previously unemployed accountant explained, "and they offered me a promotion to manage an auditing group. I was stunned. *Me?* They wanted *me* to manage this new group? That's when I realized that, even a year later, I hadn't yet quite recovered from the effects of losing a job. I still wasn't sure of my own capabilities."

As described in Chapter 3, loss of self-esteem is an almost universal response to the loss of a job. The problem is, even though you find a new job you may not recover your sense of self-esteem immediately. This effect of job loss can definitely be detrimental to your future career success.

The key to recovering confidence may be in how you look back on the experience of being out of work. If you were laid off because your previous employer was having financial difficulties, you need to focus on the fact that laying you off was a *business* decision. As you begin to realize that the company made a bottom-line decision about you, you can let go of the feeling that you somehow brought this on yourself and focus instead on moving forward in your new position.

LEFTOVER FINANCIAL CONCERNS

While you were out of work, you most likely spent a great deal of time worrying about money. Before you lost your job, you never thought twice about going out to dinner. While you were out of work you probably compared cans of corn to determine which was cheapest. This obsession with money (or more accurately, the lack of it) can tend to stay with you after you find a new job. As with unemployment anxiety, money worries can be irrational, especially if you have found a new job that offers the financial security you need.

You should be aware, though, that these new-found concerns over money can actually have a positive effect. If you have never been very effective in managing your personal finances, the experience of being unemployed has probably taught you how important this skill can be. You have likely learned that excess consumer debt in the form of high credit card balances can spell financial disaster for you and your family. Along the same lines, you now probably also realize that money in savings is not just nice to have, it can mean the difference between surviving and struggling during difficult times.

"The first thing my husband and I did when he was laid off," one woman explained, "was to cut up the credit cards. We had outstanding balances on several of them. I'm not sure why it took a layoff to wake us up to the fact that we were playing fast and loose with our finances. Six months of warning notices while he was out of work taught us to realize that these cards had placed an unreal burden on our lives. Now that he's back to work, we have one card apiece and we pay the balance every month. We paid all the outstanding balances with a home equity loan and we'll be out from under that in three years."

When you are out of work, living within your means takes on a whole new meaning. When you return to work and start receiving a salary, the financial lessons you have learned can make you and your family more financially secure, regardless of what the future brings. Some of the important lessons learned by formerly unemployed people are in the areas of:

Debt. Consumer debt can be one of the most financially destructive concepts ever invented. Not only do most forms of consumer debt carry high interest rates, they also provide painless ways to buy a lot of things you cannot afford. The high cost of excess consumer debt can be masked by your salary when you are employed. When you are out of work, the cost of the interest alone can financially strangle you and your family. "If you learn nothing else from being out of work," one formerly unemployed man asserts, "the valuable lesson you should come away with is that credit cards can eat you alive if you let them."

Savings. Many experts suggest that you should have at least six months' salary in savings to carry you through emergencies. If you don't have the savings to begin with, unemployment can be doubly painful. Most people come away from the experience of unemployment realizing that they need to have a more effective cushion against the uncertainties of the economy.

Doing without. "When I was out of work," one woman said, "I looked at *every* purchase, from a pair of shoes to a can of peas, and asked myself, 'Do I *really* need this?' It got frustrating after a while. But you know, it's really the first time I ever even *asked* the question." Obviously, if you are going to reduce debt and increase savings, the money will have to come from somewhere. If you can come away from the experience of unemployment with a renewed sense of what you can and cannot live without, you can better insulate yourself and your family against whatever financial problems the future may bring.

Controlling Your Sources of Income

Because unemployment teaches that the business world can be a fickle place, some formerly unemployed people take the experience as a cue to assume more control over their earning power. There are a number of ways to ensure your future marketability and earning power. The idea of assuming more control over your financial future may not have occurred to you before you lost your job. However, the experience can be a catalyst for changes in the way you originally planned your career.

"I used to think I'd never start my own company," one man pointed out. "I always thought it would just be too risky. That was, until I got laid off. That's when I realized that large companies themselves are full of risks. Now I'm working for another large company, but I'm still living as if I were out of work. I'm saving every dime to finance my own business in three years. At least that way my fate will be up to me. I know the risks can be pretty high for a new business, but even if I fail, I'll feel less at the mercy of some corporate decision I couldn't control."

Taking more control over your earning power does not have to be as radical as starting your own business. You may simply decide to go back to school to increase your own marketability. You may find other things you can do in addition to your job to create additional income. Losing a job can be a powerful incentive if used in the right way. One person may go on to write a book he or she had always wanted to write. Another may buy and renovate rental property in an up-and-coming neighborhood.

The point is, there are many things you can do to become less dependent on the wages provided by a corporation whose financial future you cannot control. If losing a job teaches you nothing else, it can teach you to be less complacent and more financially self-reliant. That lesson itself can be worth its weight in gold.

THE VALUABLE LESSONS

Losing a job can be a painful way to learn some valuable lessons, but you can be sure that once you've learned them you won't forget them. Two of the more important lessons, keeping an eye towards the future and controlling your financial situation, have already been discussed in this chapter. In addition to the effects on your career and financial outlook, job loss can have a significant effect on your personal life as well. In fact, many people who have lost a job quickly learn to reassess the priorities in their lives, often much to their advantage.

Owning Your Own Life

"I was absolutely committed to my former employer," one engineer recalled. "I used to routinely put in 14- or 15-hour days, and I can't count the number of weekends I lost. I'll never be that dedicated again. I look at my new job as strictly a business relationship. They pay me to do good work and in exchange I give them good work and a reasonable work week. But they don't own my life and they never will. I'm not as inclined to work late or be there on Saturday. When I was out of work, I realized how important my family and friends were in pulling me through. Now I realize that no job will ever again be important enough for me to sacrifice my family for the sake of the job."

Especially if you used to work for a large company that fostered the image of a corporate family, you may have invested a great deal of emotional energy into your former employer. If you've been through the experience of losing a job, you should begin to realize that work is something you do in exchange for a salary. You will probably never be able to give the same loyalty to your new employer because you now realize that your emotional commitment to the company didn't match their business interest in you.

"I realized I had invested my life in that place," Maureen, a formerly unemployed market researcher said, "to the point that the company became a substitute family. I'm single so I don't have a lot of family commitments, and it seemed as though they were willing to take anything and everything I could give. I found out after I was laid off that one of the criteria they used in choosing who would get the ax was whether or not the individual had a family to support. Because I didn't have a family to support, I was one of the first on the list. Now I have a new job, but for the first time in six years, I also have a *life*. I spend less time at the office and more time doing other things that matter to me."

As you can see, one of the positive reactions people have to losing a job is the realization that they don't owe their lives to their employers. After going through the experience yourself, you can come to the same realization: An employer doesn't own you. The company you work for pays you in exchange for reasonable time and effort but not for your undying loyalty and 24-hour-per-day commitment.

Volunteer

Finally, one of the most important lessons sudden job loss can teach you is that it can and does happen to anyone. You probably never expected that your career path would one day include a trip to the unemployment office, but now that it has, you realize how little difference there is between you and the rest of the people who were in line with you.

"I remember one of the three trips I made to the unemployment office when I was out of work," Maureen recalls. "All I could think about was my dad's advice when I'd once thought of dropping out of college: 'Just get the degree,' he'd said, 'or you'll never even get a foot in the door.' I thought a college degree insulated me from the world of the unemployment office. As I sat there one week before Christmas, I realized that it really *could* happen to anyone. I realized I was connected to all these people in some way, whether I liked it or not."

The experience of being unemployed, including trips to the unemployment office, should have taught you that sudden job loss can and does happen to anyone. This experience can also be a catalyst for volunteer or community work you always thought you'd get around to but could never find the time. Many people who have been unemployed and go on to find new jobs find they are more motivated to get involved with volunteer projects, some for the first time.

Soon after she found a new job, Maureen became a volunteer literacy tutor for an inner-city community center. "When I started my new job, I was really tempted to put the whole experience behind me and forget I was ever one of those people sitting in the unemployment line. But the experience taught me that there are many things in life more important than finding a new job —like helping someone *else* find a job, for instance. Doing volunteer work to help other people stay out of the unemployment line helps me remember that important lesson."

KEEPING THE VALUABLE LESSONS

If you've been through the experience of being unemployed, you've probably learned some valuable lessons. You've learned that you always need to be open to other options in your career, and you've learned to watch for signs that your current employer may be in trouble. In addition, you are probably now more aware of and in control of your financial situation. Finally, you've learned to reassess your life and decide what part of your time and energy you're willing to give your new employer, and what part belongs to you and your family.

These are valuable lessons that you may never have learned any other way. These lessons can make you more financially secure, more active in managing your own career, and more content with your personal life. Rather than try to forget the experience ever happened, you need to remember what you've learned as you focus on the future.

"No doubt about it, being unemployed was an awful experience," Maureen agrees, "but I've walked away from it with some important lessons I might not have learned any other way. I realize I own my own career now and I'm more open to new opportunities than I ever was before. I also realize what belongs to me and what belongs to the company. Granted, losing a job is not the most painless way to learn what I've had to learn. But at least I know I'll never lose those important career and personal lessons, no matter *what* happens down the road."

Index

Alimony, 108
Allen, Jeffrey G., 157, 161
Appeal hearing for
    unemployment
    compensation denial,
    91
Averbeck, Dr. Daniel H., 135

Beatty, Michael, 139, 148,
    161
Benefits, as part of severance
    package, 29
Betsinger, Larry, 2
Borrowing money while
    unemployed, 112
Burroughs Corp., 10

Calculating unemployment
    income, 98
Child support payments, 108

Children, explaining about
    job loss to, 49
Clients, discussion departure
    with, 34
Closed-door meetings, as
    layoff warning sign,
    11
*Complete Q&A Job Interview
    Book, The*, 157, 161
*Complete Job Search Book,
    The*, 150, 161
Cover letter, 147
Credit cards, 104

Depression, 44
    warning signs of, 45
Developing a family budget,
    95
Digital Equipment Corp., 1
Drake Beam Morin, 132

Early retirement, as layoff
 warning sign, 14
Executive search firms, 155

Fact-finding interview, 86
Family budget list, 96
Family budget worksheet
 two-income family, 116
 single-income family, 124
Finances, discussing with
 spouse, 67
Financial security during
 layoff, 94
Financial stability, recovering
 after job loss, 168

Holmes, Dr. Thomas, 38
Household expenses,
 reducing while
 unemployed, 102
*How to Turn an Interview
 into a Job*, 157, 161

IBM Corp., 136
Income tax, 107
Insurance while
 unemployed, 100
Interviews, preparing for,
 156

Job leads, sources of, 150
Job loss,
 embarrassment due to, 42
 impact on children, 49
 impact on family, 52
 impact on spouse, 54
 men's reaction to, 55

stress impact of, 38
 women's reaction to, 57
Job loss anxiety, 44
Job search, 131
 cost of, 133
 creating a project plan for,
  69
 defining, 137
 eliminating distractions, 70
 length of, 132
Job search criteria, 136
Job search expectations, 53
Job search expenses,
  deductibility of, 134
Job search network, 150
Jobs, Steven, 136

Lavington, Camille, 2
Layoff,
 day you find out, 23
 discussing during
  interview, 157
 emotional impact, 36
 former coworkers
  comments about, 43, 61
 preparing for, 19
 warning signs of, 6
Layoff notice anecdotes, 40
Leftover anxiety, 166
Loan payments, paying while
  unemployed, 103

Managed attrition, as layoff
  warning sign, 9
Mental health centers, 46, 72
Mergers, as layoff warning
  sign, 10

NeXT, Inc., 136
Non-essential expenses, 119, 127

Ohio Bureau of Employment Services, 80
Outplacement assistance, as part of severance package, 28

Pay cuts and deferrals, 13
Perfect Cover Letter, The, 148, 161
Pratt & Whitney, layoff announcement, 8

Qualifications, reviewing, 137

Raffaniello, Dr. Eileen, 56, 61, 67
Real estate taxes, 106
Recruiting firms, 134, 155
Reducing expenses during unemployment, 98
Reference books, job search, 161
Rent, negotiating payments while unemployed, 100
Resigning in advance of a layoff, 16
Resume example, 141
Resume Kit, The, 139, 161
Resumes, characteristics of effective, 139

Salary negotiations, 163
Savings, using while unemployed, 100
Schmidt, Dr. Marlene, 49
Self-esteem, recovering after job loss, 168
Self-esteem, impact of job loss on, 38
Severance pay, impact on unemployment compensation, 33
Severance pay, negotiating, 25
Severance pay, standards, 26
Shea, Bob, 48
Sheehan, Donald, 80
Sperry Corp., 10
Surviving without an income, 115

Target companies for job search, 139
Taxes, impact of unemployment compensation on, 93
Taxes, paying while unemployed, 105
Temporary employment, 159
Tomasco, Robert, 7
Tuition, paying while unemployed, 109

Unemployment,
avoiding in the future, 167
valuable lessons of, 171

Unemployment
    compensation,
  appeal of denial, 90
  applying for, 78
  calculating benefits, 80
  denial of, 89
  rules governing
    applications, 81
Unemployment
    compensation system,
    76

Unemployment forms, 86
Unemployment office, 74
Unisys Corp., 10
Utility payments during
    unemployment, 101

Wage Record System, 75
Wall Street Journal, 2, 7